THE WISDOM OF THE AGES

IN

ACQUIRING WEALTH

BY

WELLES WILDER

THE WISDOM OF THE AGES

IN

ACQUIRING WEALTH

is published by and available from

CAVIDA LTD.
P.O. BOX 416
5615 McLeansville Road
McLeansville, N.C. 27301

It is the intent of CAVIDA LTD. to publish
and maintain the availability of

THE WISDOM OF THE AGES IN ACQUIRING WEALTH

in perpetuity

The price is $17.50

INTRODUCTION

Throughout the ages man has contemplated the age old question "How does one acquire wealth?" **Why are some men wealthy and others who work just as hard or harder are not?** Most never found the answer to that question. In fact, most men did not realize that there was an answer to that question...those who found the answer had the secret of how to acquire wealth.

I have written this book because I have discovered this secret. The incredible thing is that I have found not one book that explains this secret in terms of our practical modern day civilization. This secret is very simple, as are most really basic and important things. The farther we stray from the essence of what a thing really is, the more complicated it becomes.

This secret could be taught in one semester to any high school student.

Why did I name this book THE WISDOM OF THE AGES IN ACQUIRING WEALTH? Why not the "secret" of the ages? The reason is, that when you finish reading this book, you may think that you always knew this secret. You really don't know it, but you may **think** you do because it is so simple. It's one thing to think you know something. It's another thing to do it. But the reality is, you don't really know it until you **do** it.

The "wisdom" of the ages implies **acting** on knowledge. The wise person learns the secret, acts on it and acquires wealth. The imprudent person learns the secret, but does **not** act on it.

I have tried to present this "wisdom of the ages" in a way that I hope will be interesting and entertaining to the point that it will command your attention. Most books I have read could be condensed by a factor of at least 70% and still convey all of the necessary information presented. There are few books that are so direct and concise that if one began to underline the important things, he would end up underlining most of the book. I have tried to make this book one of those.

Imagine now that you are a senior in high school. You have signed up for a class called "Wealth Acquisition 101." The class meets only once a week. The teacher is Mr. Richmon who, incidentally, is the wealthiest man in town. Mr. Richmon has persuaded the school board to allow him to teach this course for the first time in any school anywhere in the world.

As we glance around the room to see which of our friends have also chosen to take this unique course, the bell rings and Mr. Richmon walks into the room. There is a hushed silence of excited anticipation as the teacher sits down on the edge of the desk and surveys the class room.

SESSION 1

Mr. Richmon's presence alone commands attention. When he speaks, people listen. "The purpose of this class is to teach each of you how to become wealthy. Until now high school curriculum has included almost everything except this subject, yet this is certainly one of the most important subjects that can be taught. The problem is that few, if any, believe that the subject can be defined and is therefore teachable. I can assure you that the subject can be taught and I intend to prove it this semester."

"Let's begin by asking the age old question, **'Why are some men able to acquire wealth and others are not, even though they may work just as hard at it?'**"

Steve raised his hand, "Because some people are smarter than others."

"That may be true, but how do you define smart?"

Steve hesitated and then said, "Let's define smart as being intelligent."

"That's an interesting thought. However, how many wealthy people do you know who are intellectual giants? As a matter of fact, studies have shown that there seems to be no correlation between those who are wealthy and those who are very intelligent."

"Then let's define smart as being educated," Steve continued.

"All right, Steve, how many highly educated people do you know who are **not** wealthy? Would you say that most teachers, professors and educators are wealthy? Again, studies indicate that there appears to be an **inverse** correlation between those who graduate from college with high averages and those who graduate with lower averages...relative to the wealth both groups are able to acquire."

Vicky spoke up. "People become wealthy because they get the breaks."

"How would you define, 'get the breaks?'"

"Well, you know, they just happen to be at the right place at the right time."

"Would you say that is the same thing as being lucky?"

"That's what I mean, some people are just lucky...they get the breaks!"

Mr. Richmon smiled. "Luck is a very interesting subject, so interesting, that we will discuss it in detail in a future lesson. However, for now let me pose a question for the whole class. Do you know of anyone who attributes his wealth to the fact that he was lucky enough to win consistently at the race tracks or gambling casinos?"

Tom raised his hand, "Some people are wealthy because they inherited money."

"That's true," said Mr. Richmon, "but the key word there is **some**. That is a special situation that only a few people have.

What are some other special reasons that **some** people become wealthy?"

"Some people attain wealth because they have a special talent. For example, a movie star or a song writer or an inventor all have special talents," ventured David.

"Very good," said Mr. Richmon. Some people attain wealth through a special situation that is not available to everyone, but these special situations account but for a small segment of those who attain wealth. So we will concede that some people are wealthy because of something special that was, in essence, given to them...something that most people do not have. However, man has always known that these special circumstances result in wealth for a few, but setting this special situation aside, again, let's ask the age old question..."

"Why are some men able to acquire wealth and others are not, even though they may work just as hard or harder at it?"

"We have eliminated special situations, luck, intelligence, education, and just plain hard work. Any other thoughts?"

After about a minute of silence, Mr. Richmon said, "This is not complicated. What we're talking about here are very simple concepts. When we finish this course, many of you will think you have always known the answer to this question, so think about it for another couple of minutes."

[Before you turn the page, consider this question with the class for a couple of minutes. The answer is very simple... in fact it can be expressed in just two words.]

"The answer is simply **know how**. Some people just know how to acquire wealth. They know how either because they learned it from someone else or they learned it on their own. However they learned it, they become wealthy **because they know how to acquire wealth.**"

David raised his hand, "Mr. Richmon, are you trying to tell us that the only difference between the rich and the poor is that the rich know how to make money?"

"No, David, what I am trying to tell you, as you put it, is that the only difference between the rich and the poor is that the rich know how to **acquire wealth**. We are going to learn that making money and acquiring wealth are not the same thing. Many people make a lot of money but they never become wealthy."

"In fact, many people who earned a lot of money during their lifetime end up as poor as some who **earned** very little money. The paradox is that some people who earned very little money over their lifetime can end up being relatively wealthy."

"To become wealthy, you simply have to know how. You do not have to be intelligent, educated, talented or lucky. You do not have to get into a special line of work. It makes no difference what your job is as long as it produces income."

"And to top it all off, it is **fun**. You will delight in the achievement of the quest. While you are enjoying acquiring wealth, you will also savor the comfort and security that wealth brings. You will appreciate the independence that wealth affords. You will relish the freedom that wealth avails."

"Wealth and all it conveys is available to anyone who knows the secret and has the desire to pursue it. It has always been available since man began trading the fruits of his labors with others. The secret has not changed through the ages. Wars have been won and lost. Civilizations have risen and fallen, but The Wisdom of the Ages in Acquiring Wealth has not changed."

"Throughout human history man has pondered the question of why some are able to achieve wealth and some are not. Some learned the secret and followed it to wealth. Others took the same route without consciously defining the secret but, nevertheless, by following an innate logic that led to the same end."

"Can this great secret be defined and taught step by step in such a way that today anyone who understands it can become wealthy? I am convinced that the answer is **'yes'** and this class will be the first to have the opportunity to avail itself of this knowledge."

"In the next class we will begin to unveil the secret of acquiring wealth."

SESSION 2

When Mr. Richmon walked into the classroom there was no need to call the class to order, he had every student's total attention.

"In our first class we made a statement that few people would accept as truth. In essence, we said that **anyone** can acquire wealth if he knows the secret and has the desire to act on it. This statement implies that two separate things are necessary. **To know** and **to do**. You can learn the secret but it will be of no value to you unless you do it. You will only do it if you have a strong desire to become wealthy."

"Having made that qualification, we will now begin to reveal the secret of acquiring wealth. The secret has three parts. They are:

[1] ACCUMULATE
[2] INCREASE
[3] PROTECT

Today we will discuss the first part, **accumulate**. Accumulation can be expressed mathematically by **The Wealth Equation**. I will write it on the blackboard."

$$A = I - N$$

$$ACCUMULATION = INCOME - NECESSITIES$$

"Now let me ask a question. If income **equals** necessities how much is accumulation?"

Aaron raised his hand, "If income equals necessities then accumulation must be zero."

"Exactly," replied Mr. Richmon, **"and that is exactly why most people are not wealthy**. You cannot INCREASE or PROTECT something you don't have. You must provide your own starting point in order to accumulate wealth."

"Another way of stating that is, you must **pay yourself first**."

"What do you mean by **pay yourself first**?" asked Tom. "I have a job after school and everything I make after taxes is paid to me. I get it all."

"How long have you had this job, Tom?"

"About a year, sir."

"How much does the job pay after taxes?"

"Ninety dollars a week."

"So, Tom, ninety dollars a week times 52 weeks means that you now have $4,680. Am I correct?"

"No sir, I have about $23.00."

"But I thought you said that 'you get all the money,'" replied Mr. Richmon.

"I did get all the money, but I had to buy some clothes, a stereo tape player, milkshakes, movies and, you know, all the rest."

"So, what you are saying Tom, is that you worked a year, earned $4,680, paid a total of $4,657 to the man who owns the clothing store, the man who owns the music store, the man who owns the ice cream parlor, and you know, all the rest.

But you paid yourself only $23.00."

"Yes sir, I guess that's right, but I never thought of it like that."

"Now Tom, suppose you had paid yourself first, let's say, a portion of what was paid to you. If you had paid yourself 20% first, then how much would you have now?"

"That figures out to be $936.00."

"So, applying The Wealth Equation to this hypothetical situation means that your Accumulation for the year would have been $936.00. In order to have done that you would have had to cut your necessities by $913.00."

Vicky spoke up, "That would have been okay for Tom because he still lives at home and doesn't have to support himself. However, people who are raising families, paying rent and buying groceries can just barely make ends meet. There is no way that they can pay themselves 20% or even 10% for that matter."

"Vicky, you have just summed up very aptly the most popular misconception of the ages. If that statement were true then we would not be holding this class today...and the only wealthy people throughout history would be those who fell into the category which we previously defined as 'special situations'. That would mean that no one could acquire wealth unless he had a special talent that few people have. In other words, there would have been very few wealthy people, and worst of all there would be no hope or chance of the average person ever becoming wealthy."

"For the time remaining in today's class, I am going to try very hard to disprove Vicky's statement. If I am unsuccessful then there will be no point in this class meeting again."

"Let me begin by telling you about three actual families that I know very well. The names, of course, will be fictitious."

"Bob Brown and his wife, Sarah, have two children. The Browns are a pretty average family. Sarah has a part time job and together they bring home about $50,000 per year. Bob and Sarah each have a medium priced new car. They are members of a small country club where Bob plays golf and the kids swim in the summer. They have just bought a new home in the country club area and are making payments on the mortgage, both cars, several credit card accounts and a loan from the Friendly Finance Co."

"The monthly bills always seem to be a little more than the monthly income so periodically Bob needs to refinance the loan at the Friendly Finance Co. to catch up. As Vicky said, it takes all they can scrape up just to make ends meet. There is just no way that they can pay anything to themselves because their income slightly exceeds their necessities. If Bob missed a paycheck, they would be in trouble."

"The second family is the Greens. Bill Green and his wife Faye also have two children. Bill is a partner in the city's biggest law firm and Faye is the top producer for the most prestigious interior decorating company in town. Between them they take home $130,000 per year."

"They each drive a Mercedes and belong to the city's elite country club. They have also recently bought a new home near the country club. The children, of course attend the best private schools and a full time maid takes care of the house, the children, and cooks the meals."

"They feel it is necessary to entertain their friends and customers on a regular basis, so they usually have a catered dinner party out by the pool about once a month. Since they attend a number of their friends' parties they must continually add to their wardrobe and keep up with the latest fashions. After all, it is absolutely necessary to their business life to maintain appearances!"

"Bill and Faye have a budget and they put aside a few hundred dollars every month; however, about twice a year something unexpected comes up and the savings account is raided. They have all the payments the Browns have except, of course, bigger."

"They know they are going to have to cut out something because the kids will be going to college in a few more years. Bill and Faye have spent quite a bit of time discussing where to cut, but there is just no way to save anything at this point. Maybe when the cars are paid for...! If either Bill or Faye missed a pay check, there would be a problem!"

"The third family is the Whites. Frank and Martha have three children. They live on a couple of acres a few miles from town. Frank works at a textile mill. His job is to repair and maintain the weaving looms."

"Martha pays the bills and keeps track of their financial records. She also plants a small garden in the summer. Frank clears about $25,000 per year after taxes. He drives a five year old pickup and Martha drives a three year old medium priced Ford. The only monthly payment is the mortgage. Their ten year old home is very attractive. Although they have a credit card which is used occasionally, it is always paid up every month so no interest is added. Frank and Martha never bought anything on long term credit except the house. They even pay cash for their cars and trucks."

"They also attend church every Sunday and tithe ten percent of their income to the church. In addition, they pay themselves 15% of their income every month. Occasionally they have to borrow from their savings to buy a car or pay for unexpected expenses. In the fifteen years they have been married they have kept for themselves fifteen cents of every dollar they have made. If Frank missed a **year** of work, it would be no problem."

Mr. Richmon paused and watched the expressions change on the faces of his students. There was a long silence and then Vicky spoke up.

"I see it! I see it! No matter how much money you make, your **necessities** will always equal your income. In other words you will just barely make ends meet!"

"Its like a trap," said Tom, "all you can see is your own situation into which you have gradually grown. Your necessities will always **grow to meet your income**."

"Unless," said David, "you always pay yourself first a portion of what you make. That's the only way to overcome the trap. You simply pay yourself first and **what's left** then **grows** to meet your necessities."

Wayne spoke up for the first time, "What strikes me is the word necessities. That word is a misnomer. Necessities are not just those things that are necessary to support you and your family, rather, they are also the things you **desire right now**, either for your immediate pleasure or to support the image you have set for yourself."

"Right," said Steve, "necessities are really only those things necessary to support life. For example, food, shelter, transportation, and medical care. Yet we all seem to classify necessities as everything we want at the present time."

Just then the bell rang and Mr. Richmon, with a look of satisfaction, said, "We will continue this discussion next week. You are a very astute class."

SESSION 3

As usual, Mr. Richmon was present and ready when the class filed into the room.

"In our first class we said that making money and acquiring wealth are not the same thing. I would like to show how this is so by using as an example two of our three families we talked about last week."

"The Greens made the most money, $130,000 per year. However, they kept none of it for themselves. At the rate they are going, in let's say, thirty years, they will have taken in almost four million dollars yet they will have acquired very little wealth. Most likely, the equity they may have in their house will be the extent of their wealth."

"Now, let's consider the Whites. In thirty years they will have taken in $750,000. Currently, they are paying themselves 15% of what they make. Frank plans to increase that to 20% as soon as the children are out on their own. If they pay themselves 15% of what they make for the first 20 years and 20% the last ten years, then at the end of 30 years at, let's say an average of 8% interest, they will have accumulated $484,793 dollars. By then their house will be paid off and they will be debt free. At that point Frank can retire at age 53 and draw approximately $40,000 per year for life...just off of the interest of the total amount that they have paid themselves. In addition, they will still have almost $500,000 secure in the bank. Does everyone now see the difference in making money and acquiring wealth?"

David raised his hand, "How do you define wealth... how much money is wealthy?"

Aaron replied, "If I made $25,000 per year working hard for 30 years and then quit working and received $40,000 per year and had a half million in the bank that would not diminish, you would have a hard time convincing me that I wasn't wealthy!"

Mr. Richmon laughed, "Suppose at the end of 30 years, Frank should decide to work 5 more years and continue his plan. If so, he will **be able to retire on $60,000 per year and maintain $750,000 in the bank**!

"Now that we have discussed the difference between making money and acquiring wealth, and you have had a glimpse of how fast one can accumulate wealth, by paying himself first, let's look at the Brown's situation."

"As Tom so aptly put it last week, they are in a trap...a spending trap. They spend more than they make. How can they get out of this trap?"

"First of all, they must understand what the trap is," said Steve, "and they must want to get out of it."

"Very well put," said Mr. Richmon. "They must have the desire to become wealthy. We will also talk about that in detail later, but now how about some practical ideas about how Bob and Sarah Brown can begin paying themselves first."

"They have just got to spend less," said Carol. "They have to decide what they can do without."

"Let me suggest an approach," said Mr. Richmon. "Did you know that a large portion of everything you buy is bought on **impulse**? Stop and think about it. You receive a beautifully illustrated sales catalog in the mail. The description of the product is so enticing that you really don't see how you got along up to now without it."

"Every day you are bombarded in the newspaper, magazines and billboards with new and better products...at prices that will save you money! You can hardly ever walk through a shopping mall without seeing something that you just must have."

"All of these displays are set up for just one reason...**to entice you to buy on impulse**. So, the first thing to do is to **stop all buying on impulse**."

"That sounds good, but how do you do that?" asked Karen. "It takes planning," said Mr. Richmon. "The best way to stop impulse buying is to make a list of **the 10 things** you want to buy next. Let the whole family get involved in what should go on the list. However, the person who is the head of the family should have the last word. In this case that would be Bob. It's okay to change the order of the ten things; however, a new item cannot go to the top of the list until another item has been purchased. This not only eliminates impulse buying, but it maintains a **priority on spending**."

"I'll bet that method alone could cut spending to the point that overall necessities would decrease by 5%," said Vicky.

"Probably so, but let's go on to the second step that will help. That is, stop buying on credit. The only thing that should be bought on credit is your home. We will go into why this is so later, but for now eliminating buying on credit will do two things. First, you won't buy as much if you pay cash for everything you buy. And, you can often **arrange a better price for cash.**"

"Also, the Browns are paying about 5% of their income on interest for credit cards and the Friendly Finance Co. They are paying almost 20% interest on credit purchases and loans. That's twice the rate they are paying on their home mortgage. If they stop buying on credit, eventually the existing credit will be paid off and they can begin to pay themselves the amount of the credit payment plus the **interest** they were paying on the credit.

"The last step is to set up a budget for all spending. This budget should be constructed so that within a predetermined period of time, the Browns will be living on not more than 90% of their take home income. At that time they will be paying themselves the first 10%.

"That appears to be a sound and logical solution," said Steve. "However, if you eliminate buying things you don't really need and also eliminate interest expense by not buying on credit, that alone should come to 10% of take home pay. That means that the Browns have really not denied themselves very much. Seems to me if they paid themselves their pay increases and bonuses, they would be paying themselves 15% of their take home pay before long...rather painlessly."

"It's amazing how many ways you can originate to pay yourself first if you really think about it," said Mr. Richmon. "I will tell you an innovation I came up with when I first decided to begin paying myself first. I used to buy a new car every couple of years and I knew I had a penchant for rather expensive sports cars."

"When I first constructed my budget, I decided to pay myself 20% instead of 10% within the predetermined time frame. However, I put purchase of automobiles to come out of the part I paid myself. As we have said, only the home is purchased on credit, so that meant that I would have to pay cash for all automobiles."

"Whenever, I got the urge to buy another car, I calculated how much it would cut into my plan to accumulate wealth, and it usually wasn't worth it. It's amazing how long a car will last when one is motivated to keep it."

"Our time is running out, so let me recap what we have learned today."

"First, we have learned the difference between making money and acquiring wealth."

"Second, we have learned the three step procedure for getting out of the spending trap, or to put it another way, for beginning to **Accumulate** wealth per the Wealth Equation."

[1] Eliminate impulse buying.
[2] Stop buying on credit.
[3] Construct a budget with a predetermined time frame to begin paying yourself first."

"This plan will work. It's simple and straightforward. The only thing hard about it is to **decide to do it** and follow through with it. When you decide to do it, you will find that it is hard to do only at first. After a few months, you will begin to experience the satisfaction of knowing your future is going to be under your own control. You will begin to enjoy the security that acquiring wealth provides and you will begin to feel good that you are accomplishing your plan to become wealthy. Lastly, you will know, beyond any doubt that the plan works."

Just then the bell rang ending the third session of Wealth Accumulation 101.

QUIZ #1
Sessions 1 through 3
(Answers on page 120)

There may be more than one correct answer for each question.
Circle **all** correct answers.

1. Acquiring wealth requires which of the following?

   [A] Education   [D] Luck
   [B] Intelligence   [E] Know how
   [C] Hard work   [F] Sophistication

2. Making money is the same as acquiring wealth.

   [A] True   [B] False

3. The secret of acquiring wealth has three parts.

1st	2nd	3rd
[A] Acquire	[B] Increase	[C] Produce
[D] Accumulate	[E] Income	[F] Protect

4. The wealth equation involves three of the following:

   [A] Accumulation   [D] Increase
   [B] Necessities   [E] Income
   [C] Out go   [F] Expenses

5. The wealth equation is:

   [A] $I = O - E$ [D] $I = A - N$
   [B] $A = I - N$ [E] $I = N - A$
   [C] $A = N - E$ [F] $A = I - E$

6. The basic concept of Accumulation is to:

[A] Stop buying on credit
[B] Pay yourself first
[C] Stop buying on impulse
[D] Construct a budget
[E] All of the above

7. Which of the following substantiates the most popular misconception of the ages?

[A] It takes every cent we make just to make ends meet.
[B] If we made more money we would have enough to pay ourselves first.

8. Circle the three steps necessary to get out of the trap most people are in.

[A] Stop buying on credit
[B] Let the family get involved
[C] Eliminate impulse buying
[D] Decide what you do not need
[E] Set up a special budget
[F] Understand the situation you are in

9. The hardest thing to do is:

[A] Continue to follow the plan
[B] Understand the plan
[C] Decide to do it

10. The immediate benefits once you begin are:

[A] Satisfaction knowing your future is under your own control
[B] Beginning to enjoy the security that acquiring wealth provides
[C] Knowing that the plan really works

SESSION 4

When the class filed in Mr. Richmon had just finished drawing a diagram on the blackboard. When everyone was seated he began the class with a quick review.

"We have ascertained to everyone's satisfaction that anyone can become wealthy if he knows the secret and has the desire to do it. We have said that the secret has three parts, which are:

[1] ACCUMULATE
[2] INCREASE
[3] PROTECT

"In our last session we learned how anyone or any family can break out of the spending trap and begin to ACCUMULATE wealth. The process of accumulation must continue as long as you are earning money. When you retire or for some reason stop earning money then you are no longer accumulating money according to our definition. At that time you are only concerned with INCREASING and PROTECTING your wealth."

"While you are working and earning money the portion you have paid yourself is also earning money. However, we will define this as INCREASING. In other words, profits on ACCUMULATION come under the second part of the secret which we defined as INCREASING."

"For the next few sessions we will discuss how to INCREASE your ACCUMULATION. We will start with the simplest and safest methods which have the lowest return and finish with the more involved methods."

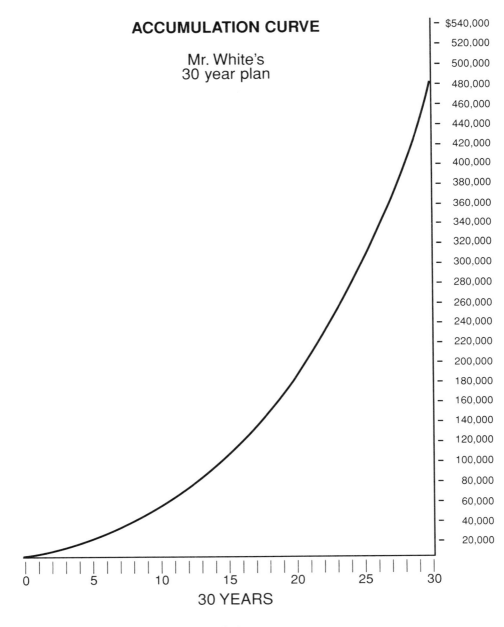

ACCUMULATION CURVE

Mr. White's
30 year plan

$540,000
520,000
500,000
480,000
460,000
440,000
420,000
400,000
380,000
360,000
340,000
320,000
300,000
280,000
260,000
240,000
220,000
200,000
180,000
160,000
140,000
120,000
100,000
80,000
60,000
40,000
20,000

0   5   10   15   20   25   30

30 YEARS

24

"The simplest and safest method for increasing your accumulation also requires the least amount of work and attention. It is the modern miracle of finance called **compound interest**. The only work and attention that is required for this method is to seek out the safest interest bearing vehicles with the highest return."

"In our last session we got a glimpse of the power of compound interest. In Mr. White's 30 years of working in a textile mill, (assuming an average annual take home income of $25,000) Frank earned a total of $750,000. By paying himself 15% the first 20 years and 20% the last 10 years (and assuming an average of 8% interest on his money) he will end up at the end of 30 years with almost $500,000 in the bank...that's two thirds of the total amount that he earned in 30 years!"

"Now let's look at the way interest is earned or if you will, compounded. On the blackboard is a graph."

"The horizontal axis (bottom line on the graph) represents time...in this case 30 years. The vertical axis represents money...from zero at bottom to $500,000 at the top."

"This graph represents Mr. White's **30 year plan** to accumulate wealth. The curve shows the increase in both his payments to himself **and** the interest on the payments. Each month the interest is added to the total which then earns interest for the next month."

"Notice that at the end of the first year, the total is 15% of $25,000 which is $3,750, plus interest on each monthly payment of $312.50 compounded throughout the year which is $140.60. So for the first year the total is 3,890.60."

"Now, let's look at the 30th year of his plan. Mr. White's payments to himself amount to 20% of $25,000, which is $5000 plus interest on the $5000, which is $187.38 **plus** interest on his bank balance. At the beginning of the 30th year Mr. White's bank balance is $442,849.28. Interest at 8% compounded monthly on that amount is $36,756.05. Therefore, his total accumulation for the last year is $5000 + $187.38 + $36,756.05 which equals $41,943.43."

"Now I will ask a question. When Mr. White first hit on the idea of paying himself first, he delayed putting the plan into effect for one year because he wanted to buy another pickup truck. My question is, How much did that truck cost him?"

Tom raised his hand, "Obviously, it cost him what he would have paid himself the first year which was $3,890.60."

"Seems to me it cost him about $50,000," said David, "because if you project that accumulation curve for another year, that's about how much it adds to the total."

"I agree with David," said Mr. Richmon. "Every year that you put off implementing your plan costs you what you would have accumulated the **last year** of your plan."

Steve raised his hand. "That certainly makes a good case for not putting off implementing your program, but, it seems to me that plan is just too easy. I mean, how much time and work goes into deciding where to put your money to draw interest? I thought acquiring wealth was going to involve some extra work and time over and above your normal job. I mean, if Mr. White's plan is to retire at age 53 with an income of over one and a half times what he was making, and a bank account equal to two thirds of the total amount of money he made during his 30 years of working, and not requiring him to do any extra work or even put any time into it...I mean if that plan is the safest one, then why go any further, that's all I need to know!"

"Now wait a minute," said Mr. Richmon, responding to the obvious enthusiasm of the rest of the class, "I understand what you are saying, but stay around long enough to learn the third part of the secret...how to PROTECT your wealth."

"Now before we move on to other ways to INCREASE your ACCUMULATION of wealth, There are some basic and general things to know about interest on your money."

"How many of you know what FDIC stands for?"

"Federal Deposit Insurance Corporation," said David. "It insures up to $100,000 of your bank deposits in each bank."

"Very good, David, and the FDIC is backed up by the Federal Government. So, one thing that must be incorporated into anyone's plan to acquire wealth through compound interest is to be sure that no more than $100,000 is kept at any one bank or savings and loan institution."

"We won't go into details regarding which institutions currently have the best interest rates because that changes from time to time and you can dig that out on your own. However, the safest place for your money, especially in turbulent times is in interest bearing investments backed by the full faith and resources of your government. In the United States one of these investments would be 90 day U. S. Treasury Bills."

"Normally, these can only be purchased in $10,000 amounts; however, there are managed income funds which deal 100% in T-Bills. These funds allow you to purchase and redeem $1.00 shares in the fund at $100 minimum amounts at any time. You will receive the current T-Bill rates on your funds less a small management fee. There is no extra charge for buying and redeeming your shares. In fact, you can simply write checks on your equity...just as you would at a bank."

"Another consideration is, that generally the higher the interest rate that someone is willing to pay you, the higher will be your risk. Remember, in this plan, you become a money lender. In effect, you let institutions use your money and you will collect rent on it. Therefore, be careful to whom you lend your hard earned money."

"Whatever you do, it is a good rule never to put all of your eggs in one basket...even if it is a very good basket like U. S. T-Bills for example. It's also a good idea not to have all your assets in your own country. Countries are ruled by politicians who have the power to change regulation, rules and laws in turbulent times. History has shown that during these times, money lenders are often separated from their money."

"In turbulent times the prudent money lender will keep his funds liquid, and distributed over several different currencies and countries...and available to move within established accounts by a telephone call or wire transfer."

These somewhat complex procedures may not be applicable to you when you first begin your plan; however, as your wealth increases, so will your knowledge about the arena in which you have chosen to acquire wealth.

Steve raised his hand, "Mr. Richmon, I think I will hang in here for the rest of the course."

We will explore these procedures in more detail when we take up the third part of the secret which is protecting your wealth.

The class laughed and clapped their approval just as the bell rang and the fourth session of Wealth Acquisition 101 came to an end!"

Mr. Richmon addresses the class. "Again this week we will discuss the second step of the wealth secret which is INCREASING your wealth. As we have said, INCREASING does not involve ACCUMULATING, it involves managing the wealth you have accumulated."

"We devoted the entire last session to learning how to increase our wealth by using compound interest. This method will always be applicable **to, a portion** of your accumulated wealth...the portion that is not currently being put to a different use. Therefore a knowledge of compound interest is applicable to any method you may employ to increase your accumulated wealth."

"In the next two sessions we are going to make a general overview of several dominate arenas in which wealth has been acquired. Arena is an appropriate description because there are many seekers in competition with each other in these areas and those who succeed either **know how** or quickly learn how."

"As an individual, you will want to choose the arena that interests you the most. At some point you may even come to the place that you would want to spend your full time and efforts in that arena."

"Now, suppose for example, you are interested in investing in land development. The idea is to find a piece of land in an appropriate location and sub-divide it into residential building lots. Since you have had no previous experience as to how to go about this, how would you proceed?"

Karen spoke up, "I think I would go to the library and read

everything I could find on the subject."

"Yes," answered Mr. Richmon, "you would want to thoroughly research the subject. Then what would you do next?"

"I would go out and start looking for some land to sub-divide," said Tom.

"There is something you should do even before that," said Mr. Richmon. "You should seek advice from someone who has been successful in that arena. Advice is something that must be sought out carefully. Everybody likes to give advice but the kind of advice you want is more difficult to get. People who have learned the hard way how to succeed tend to consider their knowledge quite valuable and are not as likely to make it available to a stranger. However, if you seek long enough and hard enough, you can usually find what you are seeking."

"Many years ago I was interested in this same arena...land development. After I had done as much research as I could on my own, I asked around and located the people who were not only very successful in this arena but had a reputation for being honest and fair in their dealings."

"I contacted one of these men who seemed to be very high on everyone's list and made the following approach."

"Mr. Moreland, I have saved up a fair amount of money over the years, and for some time I have had a keen interest in land development. In my research of the subject, I have learned that you are not only highly successful in this area, but have a reputation for being very fair and honest in your dealings. I wonder if you would be kind enough to spare me a few minutes of your time at your convenience. I would like to ask you several questions and possibly your advice on a couple of things. I know that your time is valuable, but I would be most grateful for this opportunity."

"Now, class, if you were Mr. Moreland would you grant me an interview, and if so, why?"

David spoke up, "If I were Mr. Moreland, I suppose I would have received a lot of requests like yours, but I believe I would have responded favorably in your case. The reason is because you had qualified yourself to receive the advice because it was obvious that you had done your homework, and even more importantly, you had the money ready **now** to act on the advice you received."

"Very good, David," said Mr. Richmon. "Mr. Moreland did grant me the interview and I believe primarily for the reasons you stated. I was somewhat surprised when I arrived at Mr. Moreland's office because I knew he was one of the wealthiest men in the county. His office was in a small room behind a country store. It was clean, but very plain. His bookkeeper was an elderly lady with a no-nonsense look and the typewriter on the desk would have been at home in a museum."

"I knew immediately that I had come to the right person for advice. When I left an hour and a half later, I knew among other things, that Mr. Moreland started on the road to success in the middle of the depression with a fourth grade education, an acre of land, a mule and an ancient saw mill held together with bailing wire. He cut the timber from his land and then sold the timber and the land and made a payment on five acres of land...and he was on his way!"

"What I learned that day about land development and money

management was equal to a lifetime of experience in that arena. I will always be grateful to Mr. Moreland for sharing his wisdom and knowledge with me. Just before I left, he said, with a twinkle in his eye, 'Mr. Richmon, do you know what a self-made man is...well he is a person who has forgotten all the people who helped him along the way!' Much can be learned from wise men who have proven that they are successful in their field."

"On the other hand, pay no attention to those who give advice unless, as Mr. Moreland put it, 'They have the corn in the crib.' If you are sick, see your doctor, but don't take his advice on investing in diamonds."

"Now that we have learned a wise and age old procedure which should be used in any arena in which we may want to invest, let's talk about an arena that has made many people wealthy."

"That arena is **Real Estate and land development**. There are several reasons for this."

"First, a home, an apartment, or a place to do business are basic necessities that everyone needs at one time or another."

"Second, it is something you can invest in on a part time or a full time basis."

"Third, it is highly leveraged; that is, a small down payment will put you in control of a large amount of value."

"Fourth, it is an investment that is not eroded by inflation."

"I have a good friend who is a very typical example of how many, many, people have become wealthy in this arena."

"Although it has been a little over 20 years ago, I remember it as well as if it were yesterday. Joe Pickett came to me and said that he had decided to invest his savings in rental property. Joe was an engineer, working on a salary and he had a good knowledge of basic construction, electrical wiring, etc."

"The very next day he bought a rundown unoccupied duplex that was structurally sound. He made a 10% down payment and financed the rest with a savings and loan institution. Doing the work himself in the evenings and on weekends, Joe soon had both apartments renovated and rented. His first step into Real Estate had been a success."

"Next, Joe made a down payment on a rather large but somewhat rundown house in a nice neighborhood. Again, Joe put the house in top condition doing most of the work himself but subcontracting a part of it. A few months after Joe bought the house, he sold it at a nice profit."

"With the profit on the house and the income from the duplex, Joe then bought a four unit apartment house (again with a 10% down payment) that also needed some work. He fixed up the apartment complex and sold it again for a good profit."

"Soon Joe had made a down payment on a 12 unit apartment complex. This time he subcontracted most of the work it took to renovate the complex. While this was being done, Joe found a piece of land, not far from the country club, that was wooded and zoned appropriately to make four residential building lots. The land was offered at a very reasonable price because it was anything but level. Other builders had looked at it and decided that it was not suitable to subdivide into but two lots. However, Joe liked a challenge, and with his engineering experience, figured out how to subdivide the land into four lots in such a way that the lay of the land actually enhanced the lots."

"Again, Joe financed the land with a small down payment and began to build a house for himself on one of the lots. Joe subcontracted most of the construction of his new house and by the time it was completed, he sold his current house at a nice profit and moved into the new house. When it became apparent how good Joe's house looked on the irregular wooded lot, he soon had sold the other three lots with the provision that he would build the houses for the new lot owners."

"Joe now had three houses lined up to build and the income from a total of 14 apartments. This put Joe on a subsistence level* and gave him the confidence to quit his engineering job and go into the construction business full time. His wife, Penny, answered the phone and kept the books."

"Next, Joe bought some land and built a 40 unit apartment complex which he rented out completely by the time he had finished the complex. The banks were glad to provide the financing Joe needed because he had demonstrated that he knew how to make a success out of everything he did."

"Over the years, Joe continued to increase the number of apartments he owned and also continued to find good land to subdivide. Joe was always careful to go slowly and never overexpand in the good times. He never had a fancy office and he always kept his overhead to a minimum."

"Today, Joe is a multi-millionaire. Although he still drives a pickup truck and keeps a hands-on approach to managing his properties, he now builds only for himself and he takes a lot of time off to hunt, fish and travel."

"I expect that almost everyone in this class knows someone who has become wealthy in this arena. The potential in this arena is great for the person who knows the wealth secret."

"We will continue this discussion on Real Estate next week."

The bell signaled the end of the fifth session of Wealth Acquisition 101.

* Defined under Glossary of terms, page 172.

SESSION 6

Mr. Richmon addressed the class. "Today we will continue our discussion on Real Estate. No other field offers the potential for acquiring much wealth in as short a period of time as the Real Estate arena does."

"Last week I told you about how my friend Joe Pickett made it in Real Estate. This week I would like to tell you how another friend did it in a somewhat different way."

"Dr. Kevin Sawyer is a general surgeon. He does not have time nor the inclination to repair old houses or take a hands-on approach to maintaining and leasing Real Estate. So, he utilizes those who are already in the Real Estate business."

"Kevin decided he wanted to begin by subdividing appropriate land for residential building lots. Since he had decided to use the services of those already in the business, he talked to a number of Real Estate agencies in his area. He was seeking advice on how to get started, but he was also evaluating each agency as to their expertise in their particular area of interest."

"After a number of interviews, he zeroed in on three that seemed to be the most knowledgeable. Then he had his attorney check out the three as to their reputation and history of honesty and fair dealings. The agency that came out on top was the Bill Davis Agency. Kevin was also particularly impressed with Bill Davis. Thus began a long and profitable business relationship for both Kevin and Bill."

"The first thing that Kevin did was tell Bill that he was ready to purchase an appropriate piece of land to subdivide into residential lots. He told Bill that if he could find land which could be bought for a reasonable price, that was not on the

37

market, that he would pay him a 5% finder's fee. In addition, he would list the developed lots with Bill's agency. If the land they were looking for was already on the market, then Bill shared the commission with the listing broker. Either way, Bill would end up selling the developed lots for Kevin."

"In a couple of weeks, Bill called Kevin to say he had found five acres in an excellent location, but it would have to be rezoned to residential. Bill explained that he could arrange for the seller to accept an option* on the property of 2% of the sales price to hold the land for rezoning. If the rezoning failed, Kevin would get his option money back in full. To insure this, Kevin's attorney would hold the option money in escrow*."

"Bill had also arranged for Kevin to take possession of the property for a 10% down payment and the seller would take back the mortgage himself with annual payments of 10% plus interest. The key to the deal was that Bill had also arranged with the seller to release any portion of the land at 150% of its prorated value."

"Wait a minute," said Tom, "You just lost me. Please explain the key to the deal in ordinary English."

"Glad you asked, Tom. Anytime anyone doesn't understand any terms I use, please stop me."

"Suppose Kevin had bought the land, subdivided it, put in streets, etc. and he wanted to sell the first lot. Without the key agreement, Kevin would have had to pay off the entire balance owed on the land before he could sell that first lot. The prorated release means that if the lot was a half acre of the five acre tract, and the existing mortgage was $100,000, then the prorated value of the half acre would be $10,000. That half acre would be released from the mortgage for a payment of $15,000 which is 150% of the prorated value."

"Next, Kevin had his attorney recommend a civil engineering firm to draw the plans for the subdivision. This included layout of streets and gutters, residential water and sewer layout. It also included hook up with the city system, storm sewers, street lights, etc. All of the specifications must be in accordance with the city zoning regulations."

"While these drawings were being made, Kevin had his attorney schedule their request for rezoning before the city planning board. When the hearing came up, Kevin's attorney presented their case for rezoning using the engineering drawings." (Obviously, Kevin's attorney expected the rezoning to pass or else Kevin would not have taken the option on the land in the first place.)

"Kevin then retained the civil engineering firm to let bids for the streets, sewers, etc. They would award the bids and then follow up and check each contractor's work. When acceptable, they would notify Kevin that payment to the subcontractor should be made."

"About a year later the development was completed and all the lots were sold. Kevin ended up making two dollars for every dollar he invested in the project."

"In the meantime, Bill Davis had found another piece of property for Kevin to subdivide into residential building lots; only this property contained 20 acres which would yield 40 lots. By the time the first lots were sold out, development had begun on the second property."

"When about half the second property was sold, Bill had found something else for Kevin...something different. He had found a piece of land in a good location near a new shopping center that could be rezoned for apartments. A conference with Bill, the civil engineer and the attorney bore out the feasibility of the project and determined that 45 apartments could be built on the property."

"The attorney convinced the property owner to hold the mortgage on the land himself and subordinate* it to whomever would make the construction loan* and the permanent mortgage*."

"This way Kevin had to put up a minimum amount of front money. By this time, the bankers who had been working with Kevin on his previous projects had gained a lot of respect for Kevin and the way he went about things. Every project Kevin had done had been successful, so the bank was glad to go along with him on this one even though this project was different from the others and Kevin had a minimum amount of money in the project."

"Kevin had the good sense to always play it straight with the bankers and money lenders. He kept nothing from them and they trusted Kevin to put everything on the table. Also, on each project Kevin learned more and more about the fine points of financing. After all, he had good teachers: his Real Estate expert, Bill Davis, and his attorney who specialized in Real Estate and financing."

"Bill kept coming up with new land deals and in a few years, Kevin had built and now owned over 600 apartments. Bill's agency also handled the total management of the apartments which included maintenance and rent collection."

"By this time, Kevin found himself spending most of his free time handling the paper work generated by his properties. He found an accountant who specialized in his area of Real Estate and set him up in an office with a secretary to handle the paper work and to check behind Bill Davis's management department."

"One day Bill called Kevin and said he had found a piece of land that was ideally located and could be rezoned for a small shopping center. Kevin authorized a feasibility study which resulted in a meeting with the engineer, Bill Davis, and Kevin's attorney and accountant. This time Kevin also invited his banker to attend."

"A shopping center was a different type of Real Estate project, but since Kevin's track record had proved that his team of experts had been able to handle everything they had done so successfully, the banker decided to go along on this one also."

"By the time the shopping center was finished, two other projects were under way. By now it had been only 12 years since Kevin had subdivided his first small piece of land but he was already one of the most successful property owners in the area."

"He could have quit his medical practice years ago if he had wanted to. However, he enjoyed his profession and wanted to stay with it. The amazing thing was that Kevin was able to accomplish all this in so short a period of time and not take any time away from his medical practice."

"The difference between Joe Pickett and Dr. Kevin Sawyer is that Kevin sought out and hired an expert to handle each stage of the development process. Joe saved money by doing each phase himself; however, in the long run Kevin ended up accumulating more wealth than Joe because Joe was limited to what he could look after himself."

"Both Kevin's and Joe's story are typical...not a bit unusual. People all over the country are doing the same thing. The reason I have spent so much time in the Real Estate arena is, that the potential for acquiring a vast amount of wealth in your own lifetime relative to the risk involved is virtually unequaled in any other field."

In our next session, we will explore another arena, the financial arena.

Just then the bell rang ending the sixth session of Wealth Acquisition 101.

QUIZ #2
Sessions 4 through 6
(Answers on page 120)

There may be more than one correct answer for each question. Circle **all** correct answers.

1. Review question. The secret of acquiring wealth has three parts.

1st	2nd	3rd
[A] Acquire	[B] Increase	[C] Produce
[D] Accumulate	[E] Income	[F] Protect

2. ACCUMULATING is money earned and kept. INCREASING means making profits on money accumulated.

   [A] True   [B] False

3. If you pay yourself about $4,000 per year for 30 years, to delay one year will cost you about:

   [A] $4,000   [B] $50,000

4. The advantage of buying shares in a 90 day U. S. Treasury Fund as opposed to buying the instrument direct are:

   [A] Can withdraw funds any time.
   [B] No penalty for early withdrawal.
   [C] Can write checks on account.

5. The arena that has made more people wealthy than any other is:

   [A] Land Development.
   [B] Real Estate.
   [C] Renting houses.

6. Some advantages of Real Estate are:

[A] It is easy to learn.
[B] Is highly leveraged.
[C] Can do full or part time.
[D] Not eroded by inflation.
[E] All of the above.

7. The first thing to do to get started in Real Estate is to:

[A] ACCUMULATE funds.
[B] Talk to others about it.
[C] Read books on the subject.

8. The second thing to do is to research the area in which you want to begin.

[A] True   [B] False

9. The third thing to do is to:

[A] Start looking for land.
[B] Interview different realtors.
[C] Seek advice from someone who is successful in the area you choose.

10. The main reason Dr. Kevin Sawyer was able to acquire wealth in Real Estate was:

[A] He had a good reputation with his bankers.
[B] He got good advice from Bill Davis
[C] He sought out and hired an expert to handle each stage of the development process for him.

SESSION 7

Mr. Richmon began the class with a short review. "In the last two sessions we have talked about INCREASING your wealth in one area...the field of Real Estate. First, we saw how Joe Pickett became a millionaire by beginning in his spare time and then soon making Real Estate development his full time occupation."

"Then we learned how Dr. Kevin Sawyer did the same thing by using the services of those who are professionals in the business...thereby devoting very little of his own time to becoming a millionaire."

"Today, I want to discuss the third arena for acquiring wealth...the stock market."

"There are three ways that the stock market can be utilized. I will write them on the blackboard:

[1] Speculation
[2] Investment
[3] Income

Speculation is buying and selling for quick gains. Those who speculate try to anticipate short term moves in the market and buy and sell for a quick profit. A few who are experts in that procedure claim to make a profit. By far, most people who attempt it lose."

"**Investment** is buying a stock and holding it in hope of making a long term profit. This method often has the side benefit of dividends being paid to the investor. Some investors make money...the ones who pick the right stocks and buy and sell at the right time. Over the long run on the average, the long term return on stocks is about 9% per year; 4 1/2% on appreciation and 4 1/2% in dividends.

"Income involves buying a stock primarily for the income it will produce through dividends. An example of this would be an electric utility stock. This type of stock also produces about 9% return over the long term. However, the dividend would be in the area of 8% and the appreciation in the area of 1%.

David spoke up, "Why couldn't you just buy stocks and reinvest your dividends and make 9% return on your investment, that's more than 8% compound interest."

"The biggest problem with that is that most people just haven't the personality or the patience to stick with their choice of stocks through the ups and downs that markets always follow. However, there are a few people who can do this. Some even use the ups and downs to their advantage."

"Many years ago, right out of college, I was working on a project that required the help of a mechanic. His name was Billy Jones. Although Billy had very little education he had a lot of common sense and was a heck of a mechanic. One day, we were taking a break and somehow got on the subject of stocks. Billy, who was somewhat older than I, said that he had made a lot of money in the stock market over the years."

"I must admit that I thought he was joking at first because he didn't seem to know the first thing about financial investing. When I learned that he was very serious and that he had actually made a real nest egg for himself and his family, I became very interested. Then Billy told me how he did it."

He said, "Mr. Richmon, it's about as easy as rolling off a

log. There really ain't nothing to it. About 15 years ago, the company that I was working for went public and sold stock in the company to raise money. The company gave all the employees a few shares. I never owned any stock before, so followed its price in the newspaper for a couple of years. I noticed that about every two years the stock would go down to about 25 to 30 and then go up to about 45 to 50 dollars per share. I started putting aside some money and the next time the stock went down to 30 I bought more. Then when it went back to 50, I sold it. When it went back down to 30, I bought it back."

"But then, I discovered that there were other stocks that did the same thing except at different times. So when I sold my companies stock at fifty, I bought this other stock that I had been watching which was now on its low end of the price. I soon discovered six stocks that had this kind of a cycle, so I split my money up where I am holding three of them on the way up and then I sell them and buy the other three when they get down to their cycle low. Like I said, there ain't nothing to it."

"What does your broker think about your success," I asked.

"He thinks I'm real lucky," replied Billy, "When I first opened my account, he kept trying to get me to buy the stocks he recommended. He told me all about their P/E ratios and stuff like that. I didn't want him to think I was dumb, so I just told him, 'Son, I want you to take my orders and I don't want you to tell me nothing except yes sir and no sir. After that we got along real good!"

"That sounds like a good plan," said Steve, "is that what you did, Mr. Richmon?"

"As a matter of fact, I thought about it Steve, but I figured

47

that if Billy could make as much money as he had by a simple 'no brainer' like that, then I could do even better if I knew more than he did about markets."

"So, I spent most of my spare time learning about markets. I talked to stockbrokers and others who also had an interest in this marvelous new found field. Everybody had a favorite stock and a dozen reasons why that stock was the best buy on the market. I learned all the terminology and even how to read charts of the companies price history. Slowly, I began to carefully purchase a few stocks."

"Occasionally, I picked a winner, but by and large, most of the stocks I bought either went nowhere at all or they went down. This was very baffling because it was obvious to us who had spent so much time studying the markets, that the stocks we bought were supposed to go up!"

"However, I was not easily dissuaded. I figured that I just had not learned enough about markets, so I studied harder and talked to more and more people who played the markets. But, my trading did not improve much if any. I still lost more than I made."

"Why didn't you just do the same thing that Billy did," asked Carol?

"About this time, I came to the same conclusion, so I researched many stocks and did find some that had this up and down cycle every couple of years. I bought a couple which were on their cycle lows and waited. In the mean time, my friends were telling me about how much they were making on their winning stocks. Unfortunately, they didn't talk too much about what they lost on their losing stocks. The stocks I had bought didn't seem to be moving up yet, so I sold them.

(I knew I could buy them back when they started to move) and bought other stocks."

"After a few more years of this merry-go-round, I backed away and took a good look at myself and I admitted that I did not have the personality or the innate patience to make money in the stock market. For a person who had been highly successful at everything else he did, that was a difficult realization."

"I still thought there must be a way to make money in this field. If I could not do it Billy's way or my way, then there must be some other way. It finally dawned on me that I should do what I did in Real Estate, seek out the person who "had the corn in the crib" as Mr. Moreland would have said."

"My search for a man who who had made it in the stock market led me to Judge Hattaway. The judge was now retired and so could be persuaded to talk to me. When I told him my story, he smiled and said, **'Son, instead of looking for stocks to trade, you should be looking for people who can trade stocks.** Now, I could tell you about several mutual funds that have made their investors an average of 15% return, compounded annually, for the last 30 years. I know, because I am one of them. I will tell you about only one of these funds, the rest you will have to track down yourself."

"It suddenly dawned on me that the way to make money in the stock market was to seek out those who had the best track records and pay them to invest for me. I found publications in the library which rated the different mutual funds. I even discovered there were books written about the men who had become legendary for their skills in managing these funds."

"I also found out that you don't ask your broker which funds are the best, you do your homework yourself and you learn the difference between load and no-load funds.

Tom raised his hand, "Funds also go up and down with the markets. Wouldn't it be a good idea to let your money collect interest until the value of the fund goes down so as to invest in it at a lower price?"

"Glad you asked that, Tom, because I have some information on that subject that I think you will find quite amazing. Statistical research on the New York Stock market from 1926 to 1983 shows that if you had predicted every top and bottom with 100% accuracy that you would have had an average annual return of 18.2%. If you were 70% correct, you would have done just slightly better than buying and holding which would have returned 11.8% annual return. However, if you were 50% correct, you would have done worse than simply buying and holding. The major risk in trying to out guess the market is that you may end up on the sidelines while a major move is taking place."

David raised his hand, "Mr. Richmon, If you only averaged 12% return from your mutual funds, over the years and invested a certain amount of money per month like an annuity, that mounts up in a hurry."

"That's right David, 12% compounded annually would generate over four times as much as 6% compounded annually and by investing monthly as you suggest, you will average your buying over a number of market up and down moves therefore eliminating the risk of buying at a top and going through a large equity drawdown until a new high is made."

Steve raised his hand. "Mr. Richmon, I have just figured out something, to become wealthy, all you have to have is know how!"

The class laughed...the bell rang...and Session 7 of Wealth Acquisition 101 was history.

SESSION 8

Mr. Richmon began the class with a short review. "So far we have talked about three arenas for INCREASING your wealth. The arena of compound interest, the arena of Real Estate, and the arena of investing in the stock markets."

"Today I would like to take an interlude from the subject of INCREASING your wealth and discuss the following three subjects which I will now write on the blackboard. They are:

[1] Risk
[2] Leverage
[3] The Value of Money

Let's begin with the last one...The value of money. To keep this discussion simple, we are going to apply a constant interest rate of 8% which is close to the average for the last ten years or so."

"I will present this question for discussion. Which would you rather have, $1,000 dollars now or $1,469 in five years?"

David raised his hand. "I think you are going to tell us that one equals the other."

"Your perception is correct, David. If you put $1,000 in the bank today at 8% interest compounded annually, in five years you will have $1,469.32. Now what does this tell you?"

Aaron spoke up, "It means that the value of money is a function of time."

"Very precisely put, Aaron. I would say that mathematics is of more than a passing interest to you. Money has a **time**

value. We could call this the TV of money. In effect, this is the amount our money will increase simply by putting it in the bank and allowing it to draw interest."

"Now, let's coin a phrase. We will call Real Profit the Profit Above Time Value. Or, for short, PATV. For the sake of this discussion, let's say that we have not had a **real profit** on our money until we exceed the TV of our money."

"Let's consider an example. If we bought something for $10,000 and five years later sold it for $15,000 how much **real** profit would we have made?"

Several hands went up but Mr. Richmon nodded to Karen.

"The profit would be $15,000 minus the TV which would be $14,693.20. In other words the real profit would be only $306.80."

"Excellent," said Mr. Richmon. "Now there is one more term I want you to understand. That is **Return on Investment**. Would anybody, except Aaron, have an idea of how to calculate Return on Investment?"

Steve raised his hand. "Return on investment would be the difference betweenwhat you paid for, something and what you sold it for, divided by what you paid for it."

"Does everyone agree with that?" asked Mr. Richmon.

This time Aaron was the only one in the class with his hand up. "You must also divide that by the time your money was invested in the item."

"Let me write that on the blackboard." said Mr. Richmon.

If   P = money Paid,
and R = money Received,
and T = Time in years,

then Return $= \dfrac{R - P}{P \times T}$

In our case, then:

P = $10,000
R = $15,000
T = 5 years

Therefore, Return $= \dfrac{\$15,000 - \$10,000}{\$10,000 \times 5}$

Return = .10 or 10%

Now let's calculate the Return on the TV (Time Value) only.

P = $10,000.00
R = $14,693.20
T = 5 years

Therefore, Return $= \dfrac{\$14,693.20 - \$10,000}{\$10,000 \times 5}$

Return = .0938 or 9.38%

David raised his hand. "Mr. Richmon, are you trying to tell me that if I bought a piece of land today for $10,000 and sold it five years later for $14,000 I would have lost $693.20 on the deal?"

"Believe it or not David, that's exactly what I'm trying to tell you. Because, if you had just put $10,000 in the bank for five years at 8% interest compounded annually, you would have $14,693.20 in your bank account. If we define **Real Profit** as PATV (Profit Above Time Value) then Real Loss is Profit Under Time Value which in your example is a minus figure...as you say, a loss of $693.20!"

Tom spoke up. "I know a lot of people who think they made a profit on a deal whereas they really lost money on it. Wait until I tell my father how much he really lost on some stock that he bought five years ago and just sold last week for what he thought was a big profit!"

Steve spoke up. "Mr. Richmon, I am amazed at what I have learned so far in this class. And, it's so simple that, as you said, we tend to think we always knew it. I'll bet there isn't one person in a thousand that really knows just what we have learned today."

"Don't go away, Steve, it gets even better. The next thing we are going to talk about is **Leverage** and how, by using leverage,we can considerably increase our Real Profit and our Return."

"Let's use the example David mentioned where he bought a piece of land for $10,000 and five years later sold it for $14,000. It turned out that he had a Real Loss on the deal of $693.20."

This time let's say that instead of buying the land outright that David bought an Option* to buy the land at $10,000 for five years. Let's say that David paid $1,000 for the option. At the end of five years, David found a buyer for the land at $14,000, just as before. David then sold the buyer his option for $4,000 and the buyer paid the seller $10,000 so that he ended up paying $14,000 for the land."

"Now, how much Real Profit did David make?"

David spoke up, "I didn't lose money on this deal! In fact, I made a Real Profit of $3,000 less the Time Value (TV) of $1,469.32 which equals a profit of $1,530.68."

"Exactly," said Mr. Richmon. "Now what was your return on the investment?"

"The return for the five year period was the profit, $3,000, divided by the money paid for the option which was $1,000 which comes out to be 300%. Now dividing that by the time in years, which is 5, gives a Return of 60%."

"Correct. That example demonstrates the power of leverage. Can anyone define what is meant by leverage?"

"To put it simply," said Tom, "leverage means controlling a lot of money with a little money."

"That's right," said Mr. Richmon, "but there is something else that goes along with leverage and its name is RISK. The higher the leverage the greater is the risk. As we have seen, leverage dramatically increases profit, or if you will, reward. Risk is in direct proportion to reward. The greater the reward, the greater the risk."

"For example, if David had not been able to find a buyer for the land within five years, then he would have forfeited his option and his $1,000 would have been lost."

"However, risk is always a necessary consideration in any investment. **Without risk there is no chance of gain**. Everything you do involves risk of some sort. Every time you

56

drive a car or cross the street, you are taking a risk that you may get hurt. Life itself is a risk. Becoming wealthy also involves risk. The idea is to keep risk in proportion to reward and always remember that if the profit is unusually high, so is the risk."

"**Never try to push your profits to unusual extremes**...the risk is always too great. You may do it once or twice, but just as surely as betting double or nothing, you will be wiped out sooner or later...and more likely sooner!"

Aaron raised his hand. "Mr. Richmon, is there some way to calculate risk?"

"There is no exact way to calculate risk because by definition, risk is an unknown. There is a rule of thumb, however, that will tend to moderate your affinity and your aversion to risk. This rule of thumb incorporates risk into an equation which results in a number which I will call the PROFIT FACTOR or PF for short. I will write the equation on the blackboard."

$$PF = \frac{\text{EXPECTED PROFIT X ESTIMATED CHANCE}}{\text{AMOUNT RISKED}}$$

"Let's apply the equation to David's option. David risked $1,000 for the option. Let's say David expected a profit of $3,000 and he estimated that there was a 75% chance that he could sell the option for that amount of profit within five years. Here is the PROFIT FACTOR equation for David's situation."

$$PF = \frac{\$3,000 \text{ X } .75}{\$1,000}$$

$$PF = 2.25$$

"What does that number, 2.25 mean?" asked Tom.

"A PF of 1 is like the result of flipping a coin. If you do it enough times, in the long run you will break even. A PF of less than 1 means that in the long run you will lose. A PF of greater than 1 means that in the long run you will win."

"I have an example," said Steve, "Let's say the AMOUNT RISKED is \$1,000 and the EXPECTED PROFIT is \$10,000 and the ESTIMATED CHANCE is 50%.

$$PF = \frac{\$10,000 \times .50}{\$1,000}$$

$$PF = 5.0$$

"Let's try my example," said Ken, "Let's let AMOUNT RISKED = \$1,000 and the EXPECTED PROFIT = \$2,000 and the ESTIMATED CHANCE = 90%.

$$PF = \frac{\$2,000 \times .90}{\$1,000}$$

$$PF = 1.8$$

"I think I would rather be 90% sure of doubling my money than be 50% sure of making 10 times my investment." said Aaron.

"Not me," said Tom. "I'll take a 50% chance any day to gain 10 times the money I risked."

"It all depends," said David. "If I were risking say, 20% of my available capital on a situation that seldom comes up, I would agree with Aaron, I would rather be 90% sure of winning. However, if I were risking say, 5% of my available capital on a situation that is often available, then I would agree with Tom because the odds are that I will make more money with a 50% risk and a 1,000% return."

"I think you guys have pretty well summed it up," said Mr. Richmon. "You must apply the equation to your particular situation and then decide whether to do it or pass on it."

"I will close this session with a well known axiom. If something seems to be too good to be true, it probably is!"

SESSION 9

When next the class filed into the classroom they each found a packet of papers at their seats. When everyone was seated, Mr. Richmon began.

"In our last session I pointed out that $1,000 compounded annually at 8% for five years became $1,469.32. If you are going to utilize the concept of **Real Profit**, which we have defined as profit over and above what money will earn at interest, then we must have a quick and easy way of calculating the future value of money."

"Fortunately, there is a quick and easy way to do this and it requires nothing more complicated then multiplication. You simply look up the interest rate and the corresponding time the interest is in effect and multiply that number by the present value of the investment."

"I have given each of you four sets of interest tables. Each set will apply to one of four situations you will be involved with in acquiring wealth. The first situation is the problem I proposed today. The solution to the problem is called...

Amount of 1 at Compound interest

The equation is $S = (1+i)^n$. For some reason, statisticians use the letter S to represent future value. The rest of the equation doesn't concern us because we are going to use a simpler equation. Our equation is simply S= A, times C, where:

$$A = \text{Present value of money}$$
$$S = \text{Future value of money}$$
$$C = \text{A constant from the table}$$

(Note: The four sets of interest tables are in Appendix I beginning on page 121. Also included are examples of the four different types of interest problems you will need to know how to solve as you begin to acquire wealth.)

Our simplified equation is:

$$S = AC$$

Where A = $1,000, the present value, and C = a constant, which can be found in the table on page 135. The constant is found by first finding the column headed by 8% which is the interest rate. Now, find the column headed by the letter n and move down to the line 5 which represents the time at interest, which in our case, is 5 years."

8%	n
1.0800 0000	1
1.1664 0000	2
1.2597 1200	3
1.3604 8896	4
1.4693 2808	5
1.5868 7432	6
1.7138 2427	7
1.8509 3021	8

"Our Constant, C, is then the number 1.4693 2808. Substituting in the equation we have:

$$S = AC$$
$$S = \$1,000 \times 1.4693\ 2808$$
$$S = \$1,469.32$$

That's as difficult as it gets. All you have to do is choose the correct equation, substitute your values and multiply by a constant given in the table."

Karen raised her hand. "That problem shows how to find the future value of any amount of money based on the interest rate and the time. What are the other three situations that we will need to know?"

"We are not going to cover the solutions to these three problems in class because they are worked out in the material passed out to you with the tables. However, I will write on the blackboard an example of the four problems so you will know what you will be able to do with the tables.

[1] Future value of a present amount of money.
PROBLEM: What will $1,000 be worth in 5 years?

[2] Present value of a future amount of money.
PROBLEM: How much money must I put in the bank today to have $5,000 in 8 years?

[3] Future value of an annuity.
PROBLEM: If I pay myself $300 per month how much will I have in 30 years?

[4] Periodic payment of the future amount of an annuity.
PROBLEM: How much must I pay myself every month in order to accumulate $500,000 in 27 years?

Ken raised his hand. "Mr. Richmon, I thought it took a knowledge of a special field of higher mathematics to find the answers to problems like that. With these tables, I can figure out in less time than it takes to write it on the blackboard how wealthy I am going to be when I am 40 years old."

62

"Exactly." said Mr. Richmon, "**It certainly gives you an incentive to pay yourself first when you know where you are going...how long it takes to get there...and how much money you will have when you arrive.**"

Mr. Richmon erased the blackboard and after a short pause addressed the class.

"Up to this point we have covered in some detail the power of compound interest, the tremendous potential of Real Estate, and the return that can be obtained by investing in the stock market with those who have demonstrated that they know how to trade the markets."

Acquiring wealth through the vehicle of compound interest requires virtually no extra time or skills of any sort. It is also the safest. Therefore, this vehicle is the standard or the basis with which to compare any other route to wealth. We have said that **Real Profit** is only what we can make over and above what compound interest will yield."

"Real Estate requires some extra time and some degree of skill but nothing the average person cannot learn as he becomes involved."

"Investing in the stock market requires some diligence in seeking out those people who have proven their skills in that arena by their track records. It also requires patience and the ability to ride out the ups and downs. The rewards from investing can be more for the time involved than either compound interest or Real Estate."

"How about starting your own business," suggested Tom, "when you have paid yourself enough to capitalize the business."

"That's the good old American dream," said Mr. Richmon. "However, today, most new businesses go broke, some succeed and manage to make a living for the owner, and a few make the owner wealthy. A government study verified that three out of four new businesses go broke within the first two years. Studies also show that a person operating his own business works much longer hours and is under more mental stress and physical fatigue than the person who works for someone else. The odds and the environment are definitely against you."

"I have also seen a study involving those who are in the area of Real Estate that we have studied. In this area, (which is not construction, but investing) three out of four are successful. That makes the odds at 9 to 1 in favor of making it in Real Estate as opposed to making it in your new business."

"The biggest problem is that starting your own business will invariably take everything you have paid yourself. **It is usually an all or nothing situation.**"

"That's a pretty dismal scenario for the great American dream, Mr. Richmon," responded Tom. "Isn't there some instance where you would recommend that a person start his own business?"

"Glad you asked that, Tom. As a matter of fact, a number of years ago, I did recommend that someone start his own business."

"His name is Bob Tillman, and at the time he was the plant manager for a large metal fabricating shop. One day Bob stopped for gas at a service station and the attendant told him that he needed a quart of oil. Bob noticed that the attendant walked back to the store room, brought out a quart of oil, put it in the car and then threw the empty can in an ugly garbage can in the island between the otherwise tidy gas pumps."

"Bob began to picture in his mind a good looking double sided display stand for the new oil cans with a removable bin inside the stand for the empty cans. Spring loaded doors on each side of the stand allowed the empty cans to be disposed of and hidden from view."

"Bob did some checking and determined that nothing like his imagined display - disposal stand was available. Next, Bob drew the plans for the stand and obtained a patent on it."

"At this time Bob came to me to ask my advice on how he should proceed from here. Bob had made pro-forma operating statements* and financial projections covering every phase of starting his own manufacturing operation. His entire savings provided for half of the required capital and his brother-in-law, who was a manufacturers' representative for similar products, offered to put up the other half of the capital and sell the product. The brother-in-law wanted a third of the stock in the enterprise for this."

"I suggested that Bob would probably make more money with less risk and without involving much of his time if he went about it another way. I suggested that he license several large companies who were already in the business of supplying equipment to service stations to make and distribute his produce. Bob would be paid a royalty for each stand that was sold."

"Bob replied that he had considered that and he agreed that it was safer; however, he had been running a similar business for someone else for 15 years and he had always wanted to run his own business for himself. He enjoyed working and the thought of retiring bored him. This was his once-in-a-lifetime chance to really do what he had always wanted to do. However, if I thought that he would not be able to make it on his own, then he would take the route I suggested. I asked Bob to leave his financial data with me for a few days and I would call him. My analysis indicated that Bob's projections were not only realistic but also on the conservative side."

"The next day I called Bob and said 'Bob, I think your chances of success are excellent.' Now, ten years later, Bob works 12 hours a day and loves every minute of it. His business is even more successful than either he or I had anticipated."

"Now, class, why do you think Bob was successful?"

David raised his hand. "I think one reason is that with fifteen years' experience running a similar business, what Bob was getting into was not really new to him. He knew what to expect from his experience."

Steve spoke up. "I think the main reason was that he had a product that no one else had and he had it patented so that he eliminated the competition for a while."

"I think another reason," said Ken, "is that the one area where he needed help was the area in which his partner was already experienced, which was sales and distribution. His partner was motivated to produce because he had an equity interest in the business."

"It seems to me that a very important factor was that Bob had the necessary capital to get the business off the ground," said Aaron.

Just then the bell rang.

Mr. Richmon was obviously happy with the class response. "We will summarize the points you just brought out at the next class."

Thus ended the ninth session of Wealth Acquisition 101.

There may be more than one correct answer for each question. Circle **all** correct answers.

1. Real Profit is the profit on a sum of money in excess of the profit from compound interest.

   [A] True   [B] False

2. Which equation expresses Return on Investment? Where: R = Money Received, P = Money Paid, T = Time

   [A] Return = $\dfrac{R - P}{P \times T}$ [B] Return = $\dfrac{R - P}{P}$

3. A rule of thumb called Profit Factor is expressed in the following equation.

   $$PF = \frac{\text{EXPECTED PROFIT X ESTIMATED CHANCE}}{\text{AMOUNT RISKED}}$$

   [A] True   [B] False

4. Which of the following is generally NOT true?

   [A] Higher profit = higher risk.
   [B] Higher leverage = higher risk.
   [C] Higher leverage = lower profit.

5. The safest and easiest way to acquire wealth is by way of:

   [A] Investing.
   [B] Real Estate.
   [C] Compound interest.

68

6. The secret to acquiring wealth by investing is to:

[A] Invest with those who have the best track records.
[B] Buy low and sell high.
[C] Seek advice from your broker.
[D] Research the markets.

7. Which of the following is the most risky?

[A] Investing in mutual funds.
[B] Real Estate.
[C] Starting your own business.

8. The best plan for investing in the stock market is to invest so much per month.

[A] True   [B] False

9. The biggest problem with starting your own business is:

[A] You will work longer hours.
[B] It is usually an all or nothing situation.
[C] It is more stressful.

10. Which one of the following will be the most important to one who wants to acquire wealth?

[A] Apply the risk equation to every investment decision.
[B] Become well versed in the field of economics.
[C] Learn to use **all** of the interest tables in this book and utilize the concept of Real Profit.

SESSION 10

Mr. Richmon began the class where the last session had ended.

"In our last class we asked the question as to why Bob Tillman was successful in starting his own business. I will try to summarize your answers on the blackboard."

[1] Bob had previous business experience in the field into which he was getting.

[2] He had a unique product with a ready market.

[3] He had protection against competition.

[4] He had help from an equity partner in the one area where he lacked experience.

[5] He was adequately capitalized.

"The point I am trying to make is that there are situations in which the odds **are** in favor of starting a new business. For example, if you have most of the above reasons on your side. However, starting a new business is the biggest gamble one can make because **it is usually an all or nothing investment**. Invariably, it will take all of the wealth you have acquired to do it. It is putting all your eggs in one basket."

"In Real Estate or any other endeavor you should always be on guard against letting yourself get into a situation that **any one project or investment can have the potential of wiping you out**. Real Estate should be diversified into a number of different pieces of property, so that if one or even several are not profitable, then it will not endanger your entire business."

"Mr. Richmon," said Steve, "Wouldn't a franchised business be less risky?"

"It all depends, Steve. I would say that franchises fall into two categories: unestablished and established. Or you could say new and old. A new franchise may require less front money but by definition it is unproven and therefore presents a high degree of risk. An old established franchise like a McDonalds for example, is less risky, but the buy-in cost is quite high."

"If you buy a franchise, you are in a **controlled environment**. The franchise is worked out very carefully to give you a reasonable return on your investment, but that's it...the potential to expand and develop the business is not under your control. You have the responsibility, the personnel problems, the headaches and long hours associated with running a business. It may make you a living, but you will only become wealthy by paying yourself first from the profits of your business and investing the proceeds just as you would do from whatever job provides you a living."

"It appears to me that you would acquire more wealth in the long run if you just left the rather large amount of front money required to buy the franchise to accumulate," said Wayne, looking at his set of tables. "For example, $100,000 at 8% for 30 years is more than a million dollars."

"So much for going into business on your own," said Mr. Richmon. "That brings us to other areas to investigate."

"How about gold as an investment?" said Karen.

"Gold does not pay interest." said Mr. Richmon. "Gold is a good investment only when it appreciates faster than compound interest. In normal times, gold will not appreciate enough to give you a **Real Profit**. There are times, however, when you should invest in gold. The extent of your investment depends on how bad you perceive the times to be."

"An understanding of the role of gold relative to protecting your wealth is essential and we will cover that in a future session."

"How about diamond rings and gold jewelry as an investment?" said Carol.

"That comes under the category of 'life style' investments and includes such things as silver service and china, etc." said Mr. Richmon. Although diamonds may be a girl's best friend, life style investments are very low on the list as far as return goes. When you walk out of a jewelry store with a diamond ring, you would do well to be able to sell it that same day to anybody for half of what you paid for it."

"Life style investments should not be bought as investments but rather for their esthetic value or just because you enjoy them."

"How about insurance?" asked Steve.

"There are as many different insurance plans as there are insurance companies. Some are designed for a special purpose and some are more general. Since this is such a vast field, let's talk about the two traditional kinds of insurance: term and ordinary life," said Mr. Richmon.

"Term insurance is true insurance. It simply pays you a lump sum if you die while the insurance is in effect. It is the least expensive insurance you can buy and pays out the largest benefit relative to the premiums paid for it."

"For example, suppose you are 25 years old and you purchase a $100,000, 20 year level term policy which costs you $300 per year. Your premiums come to a total of $6,000. However, your real cost is $13,729 because that is what you would have had in the bank if you had paid the $300 per year to yourself. So, in effect, you have bought a certain amount of protection for your family for 20 years."

"That is the only kind of insurance that should be considered by the person who wants to acquire wealth...temporary protection until you have acquired enough wealth to take care of your family in the event of your death. Anything beyond term insurance is, in effect, an investment."

"For example, suppose you buy a 20 year paid up, ordinary life policy with a face value of $100,000. In this case you are insured as with the term policy for 20 years, but in addition, your policy is paid in full at the end of 20 years, and you will continue to be covered until you die; at which time your family (or beneficiary) will be paid the $100,000. The cost of this policy (at the same age as above) would be in the neighborhood of $350 **per quarter**. As you can verify from your tables at the end of 20 years you would have paid in $67,820."

"The $100,000 **term insurance** policy for 20 years has been covered by the $13,729. In addition you have paid the insurance company $54,091 of the $100,000 to pay to your family when you die."

"Wait a minute," said Ken, "who gets the interest on the $54,091 until you die?"

"The insurance company, of course." said Mr. Richmon.

Aaron was looking at his tables, "If you are age 45 at the

end of 20 years and you live to be the average age of 75, then your $54,091 that you paid in will be worth $544,299.17."

David spoke up, "Mr. Richmon, according to my tables, if I pay $300 per year for 20 year level term insurance and then pay myself an insurance premium of $516 per quarter for 20 years, at that time I will have accumulated the $100,000 face value of my policy. **Then I am my own insurance company**. Then **my family** will receive the $100,000 plus the interest on $100,000. If I live to be 75, my family will recieve more than **ten times** the $100,000 face value of the insurance policy. To be exact, my family will recieve $1,006,265.69!"

"You got it, David".

"You know", said David, "I'll bet there is not one person in a hundred that understands that concept. I always thought that the benefits of the policy were more than you paid for the insurance. Understanding the power of compound interest and the definition of **Real Profit** has to be the most important concept I have ever learned."

"It could be, David, but only if you actually **use** it. Remember, when you finish this course, you are going to think you always knew these things."

"Next week we are going to talk about **what not to do** with the funds you have accumulated."

The bell rang thus ending the tenth session of Wealth Accumulation 101.

SESSION 11

Mr. Richmon addressed the class. In our second session we established that the secret of acquiring wealth has three parts which are:

[1] ACCUMULATE
[2] INCREASE
[3] PROTECT

"Today we are going to begin discussing the third element of acquiring wealth...PROTECT."

"Protecting your wealth can be divided into three areas: protection against **other people**, against **governments**, and against **yourself**. We will begin with **other people**."

"In 1919 in Boston, an Italian immigrant named Charles Ponzi originated a scheme to extract money from the wealthy. He persuaded several well-known business men to invest in a plan he had developed to trade world currencies. Within a matter of weeks, Ponzi proclaimed big profits and paid the business men what he said were profits from his trading plan. He claimed the profits from their investments would continue at a very high rate of return."

"Before long the original investors had spread the word of their good fortune to their friends who also invested with Ponzi. They too, received extraordinarily high profits on their investments. They also told their friends and before long even the newspapers were extolling the genius of Ponzi's investment strategies. More and more money rolled in for Ponzi to invest at a faster and faster rate."

"Suddenly, Mr. Ponzi was nowhere to be found. An

investigation was initiated and it was determined that Ponzi had never invested any of the money he was given. He and a few million dollars had simply disappeared."

"I see what happened," said Karen, "Ponzi paid the investors a profit from their own money in order to attract more and more money until he absconded with all the new money that came in."

"And that would have been the bulk of the money," said Aaron, "because in a deal like that most of the money comes in in the last few weeks before the game is over."

"Exactly," said Mr. Richmon, "and believe it or not, that same scheme is still being played today under different names. Sometimes it involves oil leases, sometimes gold and silver and precious coins. Often, the vehicle is land, usually in a retirement area where land costs are high. Recently, a number of movie stars and some very prominent people were conned into just such a scheme and recommended it to others — just as famous people often recommend a product such as an automobile or a perfume. The scheme is often advertised in magazines and newspapers and by direct mail."

"If the scheme is pulled off so cleverly," said Ken, "how can one know to be aware of it. I mean, especially when the initial investors are making money and recommending it?"

"There are two things that are inherent in a Ponzi scheme, **high profits**, but for a **short time**. If someone tells you that they have an investment that is returning extraordinarily high profits, find out how long they have been receiving the profits. By its structure, a Ponzi scheme cannot last long because the influx of investors cannot be maintained at the maximum rate. When the rate of money input begins to decrease, the

76

crooks pack up and run. Sometimes, the authorities smell a fraud and move in even before the rate of money input begins to slack off."

"The tip off then," said Tom, "is a high rate of return for a short period of time."

"Right," said Carol, "but how long is a short period of time?"

"Some have been able to continue a year or more, but most are less than a year," said Mr. Richmon.

"A third thing to be aware of is a telephone call from a stranger. Today, the telephone call is the most productive method of selling a Ponzi scheme. I make it an absolute rule never to buy any kind of an investment that is offered over the telephone by a stranger. If the caller wants to send me more information, I tell him I am not interested but to send it anyway so that I can have it checked out by the appropriate government regulatory authority. That ends the conversation immediately."

"It's like you said earlier," said David, **"If a thing seems too good to be true, it probably is!"**

"By the way, Mr. Richmon," said Steve, "did they ever catch Ponzi?"

"Yes they did. In fact, the law usually does catch up with most people who perpetrate a fraud; however, very often little or no money is recovered. Your chances of getting your money back from a fraudulent scheme are very poor indeed."

David spoke up, "Mr. Richmon, this is really interesting, what are some other ways that people can rip you off?"

"There are many ways, David, most of which are designed to appeal to your **sense of greed**. We could never cover even a small number of them in this class, but remember, beware of a large return with a short history of profit."

"Now let's consider other investments to be aware of...this time, that appeal to your **sense of compassion** or play on your friendship with another person. In this case, the person is not trying to illegally separate you from your money...in fact, often he feels that he is doing you a great favor because he believes his scheme will make money for you. At other times, he simply wants your help because you are a friend who has the money to help him."

"I remember, many years ago, a friend asked me to co-sign a note at the bank for him so that he could make a down payment on a house. He said that the house was just what he had been looking for for years at an unbelievably low price and that he would be getting a big bonus at the end of the year and could pay the note off at that time."

"It seemed simple enough to me since I would not have to put up any money and he had it all figured out as to how he would pay it back. It would allow him to buy the house he had always wanted and it was obvious that at such a good price it would not be on the market for long. Simple enough...right?"

"Wrong! About six months later, in January, the banker called and requested that I pay off Jim's note. He had received no reply from the letters he had written to Jim, and Jim had not returned his telephone calls. I said I would get back in touch with him and set out to find Jim."

"When I found Jim at his new house, he explained that he had to use his bonus to pay for the expense of moving into the house and buying some furniture that was absolutely necessary. However, if I could arrange for the note to be set up on time payments, he could handle it that way."

"The bank agreed to do that if I would put the note in my name. When the first payment was due, the bank called and said the payment was overdue. The banker explained that it was my credit that was at stake and that perhaps I would want to make the payments and then collect from Jim."

"Guess what happened when I went to see Jim. He had another problem, but if I would make a few payments, he would be sure to pay me back and then take over the payments. After all, said Jim, everyone knew I had plenty of money and could afford to help a friend out...after all, what are friends for?"

"I went directly down to the bank, paid the loan off, and tried to write down just what it was that I had learned from this experience. After thinking about it for a while, I realized I had discovered a great precept. Would anyone like to suggest what it might be?"

"I know," said Tom facetiously, "never help a friend in need."

Mr. Richmon laughed along with the class, "Not quite, Tom, the bit of wisdom I learned had to do with **how** to help a friend."

Steve spoke up, "Instead of doing it for him, you should have helped him to do it for himself."

"But," said Vicky, "how could he have helped himself in that particular situation. He didn't have the money, and his chance to buy the house he had always wanted at that price would not wait."

"Hang on," said Ken, "Mr. Richmon was not obligated to help Jim just because Jim put him on the spot. I'll bet, if the truth were known, that Jim had done the same thing to some of his other, so called, friends also. In fact, since he was so successful in getting the money from Mr. Richmon, that might encourage him to keep on taking advantage of his friends."

"I think you are absolutely right, Ken," said Steve. "The best help Mr. Richmon could have given him would have been to tell him how to come up with the down payment himself by paying himself first. There is always going to be just the perfect house at just the perfect price when he had accumulated the money to pay for it himself."

David, who had been writing on a pad during this discussion, suddenly raised his hand. "Mr. Richmon, I think I have figured out the great axiom that you discovered from this experience. **Try to help a friend help himself, but do not let him make his problems your problems.**"

"You have indeed figured it out David. **In helping people, never allow their problems to become your problems.**"

"Also, as Ken pointed out, just because you have been able to acquire some wealth by giving up something on the front in order to have it in the end, you are not obligated to share it with friends and relatives or anyone else. Often, if you do, the recipients are not grateful for the help, but instead, may begrudge you for not helping them more. And, you can count on something else, they will be back for more!"

"This does not mean that you should not help those who **can't** help themselves," said Mr. Richmon. "On the contrary, I derive a lot of satisfaction from being able to help those who can't help themselves...but, by far, most people who ask for your help **can** help themselves. They either don't know how or they don't want to. If they don't know how, then **show them how**. If they don't want to make the sacrifice, then..."

Mr. Richmon paused and wrote on the blackboard:

DON'T MAKE THEIR PROBLEMS YOUR PROBLEMS!

Just then the bell rang and the eleventh session of Wealth Acquisition 101 became history.

SESSION 12

Mr. Richmon began the class with a review.

"In our last session we began our discussion of the third element of acquiring wealth...PROTECTION. We said that we must learn to protect our wealth from other people, from governments, and ourselves."

"We discussed two general areas involving other people...one motivated by **greed** and the other area motivated by our **compassion**. We could spend the rest of this semester discussing the aspect of protecting our wealth from other people, however, a general application of our two examples will cover most of the situations with which you will be faced."

"Now I would like to talk about how to protect your wealth from governments."

"Throughout the ages, those who govern have affected the wealth and well-being of their subjects by wars, taxes, wealth redistribution plans, confiscation, inflation and other political considerations."

"Now please don't misunderstand what I am saying. I am not implying in any way that any current governments are or are not doing or going to do any of these things. The reason that I am pointing out the most common ways that governments have affected wealth historically is so this course, Wealth Acquisition 101, will be of such a general and basic nature that it will be applicable to any time period, in the past or the future."

"We do not have to look back farther than the beginning of this century to see examples of all of these things that governments can do. In all cases, the best protection against governments is **to have options**. These options should be set up and ready to implement on a moment's notice. Let's look at some examples and the appropriate options that would have protected wealth in just this current century."

"The Russian revolution of 1917 which brought the communists to power was an example of confiscation. All private property and wealth was immediately transferred to the government. The only protection that the wealthy had was to have distributed a part of their wealth in one form or another to other stable and neutral countries and then fled Russia immediately to collect their wealth and resume life in another country."

Tom raised his hand, "How would the wealthy have known when the revolution would come and that the new ruling power would confiscate their wealth."

"That's the point of setting up options, Tom. They did not know when it would happen or the result. Let's look at the general procedure which I'll write on the blackboard."

[1] SITUATION NORMAL. Set up several foreign bank accounts in neutral stable countries. Establish a procedure for buying gold in each account. Transfer (wire) funds from one account to another to become familiar with the procedure.

[2] SITUATION BECOMES UNSTABLE. Increase your cash position by liquidating long term assets. Begin to transfer wealth to selected foreign countries. Increase foreign investments. Begin acquiring gold. Visit the foreign country that offers the best wealth protection and overall alternate life style and consider purchasing a second home.

[3] SITUATION BECOMES CRITICAL. Liquidate all long term assets. Transfer majority of funds to the other countries. Increase your gold holdings. Take an extended vacation to the country in which you have chosen to live.

"These options are not irrevocable. You have not burned any bridges behind you. If the critical situation is resolved peacefully to your satisfaction you can always resume your original lifestyle...with your wealth. For example, after World War II, Great Britain gradually increased the income tax for the wealthy to where the tax, in some cases actually exceeded the income being taxed. When the opposing political party came into power, the absurd tax rate was eliminated. The wealthy then returned to their former life style."

"These options will protect you as much as is possible in all of the situations that governments have created in the past to confiscate wealth."

"The one thing that governments control that is of constant concern to most citizens is inflation. For the time left today I would like to convey to you a basic understanding of inflation and how it relates to interest rates."

"Let's imagine that we are on an island that is self- sufficient and has no international trade with other islands. This island has everything a large country has except on a minute scale. Long ago the citizens turned in their gold to the government for redeemable gold certificates. Over the years the certificates became known as dollars and the people nor the government any longer associated the dollars with gold."

"Originally, there were just so many dollars printed and that was it. But a funny thing began to happen. The price of everything was slowly going down. This was very baffling until a college student studying economics figured it out."

"Gradually, as more people were born, the market for more goods and services increased and more goods and services were produced. Since the money supply did not expand, then the same amount of money had to buy more and more goods and, therefore, the price of the goods decreased. This made expansion very slow and difficult. Since the economy was expanding at 5% per year, it was decided to expand the money supply by 5% also. Now the prices of goods and services remained the same."

"Then someone figured that the economy would expand even more and everybody would have more if the money supply expanded at twice the rate the economy was expanding which was 10%. This resulted in an inflation rate of 5%."

Aaron spoke up. "The real definition of inflation then is that inflation is the difference between the rate of increase of the money supply and the rate of increase of the economy. However, it is only inflation if the money supply increases faster. If the money supply increases slower than the economy, then you have deflation."

"That is correct Aaron, and that is the basic concept of inflation. In reality, it is much more complicated than that because governments learned that they could borrow money by printing it. The banks came up with a fractional reserve system that allowed them also to expand and contract the current money supply. These things are outside the scope of this class, but what we do want to understand is how inflation affects interest rates because interest rates are at the heart of our plans to acquire wealth."

"Traditionally, at times when there is **no inflation** and

virtually no risk to the lender, the lender has been willing to accept between 3% and 4% for the use of his money. Let's say that in this scenario a bank will pay 3% for money and lend it, at virtually no risk, for 4%."

"Let's identify this 'no risk' rate as the **prime rate.** Now what will the prime rate be if the inflation rate is 5%?"

"That's easy," said Vicky, "The prime rate will be the base rate which is 4% plus the inflation rate which is 5%. That comes to 9%."

"Right," said Tom, "and if the inflation rate is 12%, then the prime rate will be 16%."

"You have got the idea," said Mr. Richmon. Also, if there is some degree of risk to the bank, as in the case of the average borrower, then the rate may be 2% above prime. Another consideration that affects the interest rate is the term of the loan. If the term is, let's say 20 years, as for a mortgage on a house, the interest rate will be increased because of the added risk to the bank that inflation may increase before the loan is paid off."

"When you lend your money to a bank, the interest rate you will get for your money is a function of inflation. If there were no inflation you would get about 3%. If inflation averages 5% you will get about 8%. **One of the nice things about compound interest is how the dividends increase geometrically with the interest rate.** Now for a question. If the interest accrued on $10,000 for 30 years is $22,433 at a rate of 4%, what would be the interest accrued on the same amount for the same time at a rate of 8%?"

"Steve spoke up, "Well, the interest rate has doubled so the

86

amount of interest should also double which would be $44,866."

"Wow!" said David, looking at his tables, "This is hard to believe. At 8% the interest for the same amount for the same period is $90,626. That's more than four times the amount of interest earned at 4%!"

"I've always heard that inflation is bad," said Carol, "but it appears to me that the mathematics of compound interest pretty much keep things in balance. **The higher the inflation, the higher the geometrical return from compound interest.**"

Aaron spoke up, "Obviously, the buying power of a dollar decreases as inflation increases, but this is more than compensated by the geometric increase gained by compound interest."

"There are several ways to lose money because of inflation," said Mr. Richmon. "One is to be on a **fixed income** during an inflationary period. In this case, the price of goods and services is increasing while your income remains the same. An example of this is to buy a bond with your accumulated wealth. The bond is based on the interest rate at the time of purchase and will pay a fixed amount for a specified time no matter what inflation does. It works **for** you in a deflationary period, but **against** you in an inflationary period. The same thing happens when you lend money for a long period of time at a fixed interest rate."

"A little inflation can be a benefit to the person who understands the concept; however, very high inflation has the reverse effect and stifles the economy. The reason is that if inflation is, let's say 20%, then the long term interest rate will have to be about 26%. That makes the interest so high that it is not economically feasible to borrow. When borrowing stops, the economy grinds to a halt and a recession or depression follows. There is also the danger that a little inflation can lead to much higher inflation."

"A basic understanding of the inflation scenario allows you to adjust your assets and accumulated funds to the term (time period) that is most beneficial to your accumulation plan."

Just then the bell ended the twelfth session of Wealth Acquisition 101.

There may be more than one correct answer for each question.
Circle **all** correct answers.

1. The two things we need to protect our wealth from are:

   [A] Crooks   [D] Governments
   [B] Other people   [E] Relatives
   [C] Inflation   [F] Ourselves

2. A Ponzi Scheme has which of the two following
   characteristics?

   [A] High profits   [C] Easy to spot
   [B] Makes sense   [D] Short history

3. The only kind of insurance that fits the plan for one wanting
   to acquire wealth is:

   [A] Ordinary life insurance.
   [B] Term Insurance.
   [C] Paid up annuity.

4. The great truth Mr. Richmon discovered in his dealings
   with Jim was:

   [A] Help a friend to help himself
   [B] Don't make his problems your problems
   [C] Help those who can't help themselves

5. The best protection against governments regarding wealth
   is:

   [A] Get liquid   [C] To set up options
   [B] Move   [D] Buy gold

6. If the interest on $10,000 for 30 years at 4% is $22,433, what is the interest on the same at 8%?

[A] $44,866 - Twice as much
[B] $67,299 - Three times as much
[C] $90,626 - Four times as much

7. Circle the true statements about inflation.

[A] Is caused by governments
[B] Can be beneficial if understood
[C] Produces a geometric return on compound interest
[D] Too much inflation slows the economy
[E] All of the above are true

8. Inflation can be defined as, increasing the money supply in excess of the increase of goods and services.

[A] True   [B] False

9. Except when you go into business for yourself, you should never allow yourself to be drawn into a make or break situation.

[A] True   [B] False

10. Gold is likely to be a better investment than compound interest in perilous times.

[A] True   [B] False

SECTION 13

Mr. Richmon sat on the edge of his desk and looked at the class until everything got quiet. He hesitated a moment longer and then said, "Today's discussion is going to be one of the most important sessions we have had. What you learn today will be the difference between making it and not making it for many of you who try to acquire wealth."

"Today, we will talk about PROTECTION. However, this time we will talk about protecting your wealth against **yourself**."

"Years ago I had a friend named Charlie Rushmore. Charlie was a tail gunner on a B-17 during the war. When Charlie returned to civilian life, he had one desire...to become rich. He chose Real Estate as his arena and began by selling houses to returning veterans."

"Charlie was a good salesman and soon had put aside enough money to take an option on a piece of land to subdivide. He made a good profit on it and soon found another piece of land to subdivide. Soon, Charlie had a small apartment complex of 12 units. He was on his way!"

"The next thing Charlie did was to buy a new Lincoln convertible. He quit selling Real Estate and began putting Real Estate deals together and selling the deals to some of the "big boys" in the business. Before long, Charlie became one of the partners in one of the deals he put together. Charlie was a 25% partner in a large apartment project of 100 units. To do this, he had given the group the deal he had put together and agreed to spend his full time in the capacity of the general contractor for the project."

"Charlie joined the Country Club and began mingling with

the wealthier families in town. Charlie was beginning to feel rich already. The apartment project was about half completed."

"Then several things happened that Charlie had not figured on. The cost of building materials increased, it rained almost every other day, thus slowing construction. And worst of all, several other apartment projects were coming on stream a little ahead of Charlie's project and the leasing of his apartments slowed to a trickle."

"Charlie's partners decided that each partner would have to put up an additional $10,000 to keep the project afloat. Charlie sold his own 12 unit apartment project to come up with his part of the money. Several months later, more money was needed and it was decided that each partner should put up another $10,000 to see the project through. Charlie sold his new Lincoln and borrowed all he could from the bank and just managed to come up with his $10,000."

"Several months later, still more money was needed. The partners decided that each should come up with another $10,000. Charlie tried everything, but he could not raise any more money. His "big shot" partners felt no sympathy for Charlie. They divided his share between them and hired a construction superintendent to replace Charlie."

"Charlie had lost everything he had gained in his first four years in Real Estate and to make matters worse, he owed the bank $5,000. However, Charlie knew how to put a deal together. He knew how to make a loan package. He knew construction and he was a good salesman. He would come back."

"Over the years, Charlie made a lot of deals. At one time or another, he had a part interest in apartments, strip shopping centers, and commercial buildings. One year he would be driving a new Lincoln convertible and the next year a beat-up pick up truck."

"About thirty years after Charlie made his first Real Estate deal, he came by my office one afternoon. Charlie was broke, and was trying to figure out why. We reminisced about the great deals he had put together over the years."

"I said, Charlie, what if you had just 10% of all the profits you have made on those deals."

Charlie replied, "I could retire tomorrow and not have to lift a hand for the rest of my life. I am now 57 years old and I have accumulated absolutely nothing."

And then Charlie said something else. He said, "This morning I was getting out of my car in the shopping center parking lot and another fellow who had parked beside me got out of his pickup truck."

He looked at me and said, "Mr. Rushmore, do you remember me?"

"I told him that he looked familiar."

He said, "Mr. Rushmore, about 20 years ago I was working as a carpenter on the apartment project you were building over on Bessemer Avenue. One day as I was getting off work, you were just getting into a new Lincoln convertible when I walked up and asked you a question."

I said, "Mr. Rushmore, tell me how I can accumulate some money and buy a car like that. You told me to buy a house that needed some work done on it and fix it up and rent it.

Well, I did that, and today I have 20 houses that I rent."

"I quit my carpentry job a few years ago and now I spend my time keeping up my houses. That leaves a lot of time to go fishing."

"My wife and I have our house paid for and we've put both our sons through college."

"I just want to shake your hand and tell you how much I appreciate that advice you gave me twenty years ago."

Charlie stopped and thought a minute and said, "And here I am 57 years old and broke. On top of that, I don't feel so good. Think I will stop by the doctor's office on the way home."

"That was the last time I saw Charlie alive. He had a massive heart attack in the doctor's office. He died the next day."

Mr. Richmon paused for a few moments and then continued.

"What Charlie did not realize is that he was his own worst enemy. **He was in a hurry to get rich**."

"I do not think it would have made any difference if Charlie had paid himself first, even 20% of all the money he had made. He would have invested every cent he had in his deals to get rich fast."

"Charlie is not the exception; in fact, Charlie is the rule. Most of us who want to acquire wealth want to do it fast. We do not have the patience to take the slow, sure route all the time. Sooner or later, we will see an opportunity that is a once-in-a-lifetime chance to get where we want to be in a hurry. We will risk all our assets on that one great opportunity."

"The problem is that if we win that first time, it will reinforce the idea that we did the right thing. Success, we will say, breeds more success. We will think we have learned a way to speed up our plan and we will again find ourselves in a similar **all or nothing situation and will think we can do it one more time**. We don't realize that we are on a streak which cannot continue for long. We don't realize that we will lose as surely as if we were betting double or nothing at a casino. If we do begin to see it, we will think we can do it just one more time...and then quit."

"That's why with everything he had going for him, his skills, his knowledge, even if he had paid himself first consistently, Charlie didn't have a chance of becoming wealthy...and he never knew why!"

"Now, to you in this class today. All of you know how to acquire wealth. I believe some of you will. I also believe that in spite of your know-how, good intentions and determination, most of you will not acquire wealth. If you don't, it will be for one of two reasons."

Mr. Richmon turned and began to write on the blackboard:

TWO REASONS YOU WILL NOT ACQUIRE WEALTH
EVEN THOUGH YOU KNOW THE SECRET

[1] **You will put off paying yourself first.**
[2] **You will not have the patience to become wealthy slowly and surely.**

Mr. Richmon then wrote one more line on the board and walked out of the room.

CLASS DISMISSED EARLY TODAY!

Mr. Richmon addressed the class. "In our second session, we said that there are three parts to the secret of acquiring wealth. They are:

[1] ACCUMULATE
[2] INCREASE
[3] PROTECT

As of the last session, we have completed our discussion of these three parts of the secret of acquiring wealth. In this and our last session I would like to talk about several things that do not exactly fall into any of the three parts of the secret."

"The first thing is diversification. For example, instead of keeping all of our money in the bank or the savings and loan, we could put a lot of it into other interest bearing vehicles. The return will vary according to the degree of risk we are willing to take. We know that the safer the investment the lower the return and the higher the risk, the higher the return."

"Some vehicles may pay the same return as the bank, but at the same time may offer the potential of appreciation or the risk of depreciation. Such a vehicle might be stock in an electric utility like the company which supplies your household electricity."

"Let's say that we are considering buying a thousand shares of XYZ utility company for $20.00 per share. That's an investment of $20,000. We checked certain available records and discovered that XYZ utility company has paid an average annual stock dividend of $2.00 per share for the last ten years. That's equal to 10% interest compounded annually. The bank is currently paying 8% interest compounded monthly."

"This presents a chance to diversify some of our captial at interest to a situation which is currently paying a higher return than the bank. There is also the possibility that the price of the stock will rise over the long term so that we may sell at a higher price."

"Now let's consider some other ways of diversifying. Another market that we should know about is the bond market. Bonds fall into three basic categories.

[1] Corporate Bonds
[2] Municipal Bonds
[3] Government Bonds

A bond has a face value and a fixed interest rate that it pays. The face value of the bond will vary as the interest rate varies. For example, let's say that a bond is issued at a face value of $10,000 at 6% interest for 10 years. If the interest rate stayed at 6% for the 10 year term of the bond, then the owner would receive a dividend of 6% annually for 10 years and then receive $10,000 at the end of ten years."

"If the interest rate increased to 8% during the 10 years, then the market price of the bond would decrease to about $7,500 because at 8%, a bond with a face value of $7,500 will give the same return as a bond with a face value of $10,000 at 6%."

"The purpose of a bond is to borrow money at a fixed interest rate from the person buying the bond. For example, it allows an entity to borrow money for a long period of time and pay only the interest on the face value of the bond to the holder."

"A bond is only as safe as the entity that issues the bond.

The safer a bond is, the lower the interest rate that it pays. Government bonds are backed by the full faith and credit of the federal government and therefore pay the least rate of interest relative to other bonds on the date the bonds are issued."

"The one exception to this is tax free Municipal bonds. Because the holder of these bonds does not have to pay Federal or State taxes on the interest income the bonds can pay less interest and still yield the same after profit to the holder as other bonds which are not tax free."

"All bonds are rated according to how safe they are at the current time. This information is available at your library. Corporate bonds with a low rating are referred to as "Junk Bonds". These bonds produce a very high return relative to their face value because of the risk associated with the bond. In ordinary times, Junk Bonds can produce an excellent return on investment and the chances are very good that the face value of the bond will be paid to the investor by the issuer. However, because of the risk, one would not want to invest a large part of his capital in them."

"Never hold Junk bonds in perilous or uncertain times."

"In my opinion, there is only one time to buy long term bonds. **That is when interest rates are high and you have reason to believe that the rates will come down in the near future.** Buy bonds when rates are high and sell them as soon as rates come down. Remember, bond prices go up when interest rates come down and bond prices go down when interest rates rise."

"Because inflationary periods are long and deflationary periods are short, long term bonds present more risk than money in the bank and should only be considered as a hedge against **deflation**."

"Ninety day U. S. T-Bills are short term interest vehicles and are very safe because they are backed by the full faith and credit of the government and do not lock you into a fixed interest rate, because the rate is adjusted every 90 days by a free market auction. Because of this, 90 day T-Bills are debt obligations to hold in uncertain or perilous times."

"**Gold is the only asset that is not someone else's liability**. Gold does not depend on anything or anybody, therefore, Gold is the safest investment of all. But the ultimate in safety pays the ultimate least interest...zero.

"There are a number of other interest vehicles which can be used for diversification, such as Certificates of Deposit issued by your bank for a fixed period of time at a fixed rate. Vehicles with a shorter time frame are called Bank Repros. There are other interest bearing vehicles that are available, but most of your cash assets should be in instruments that are designed for safety."

"Real Estate is another area of diversification for everyone. First, I would recommend that everyone own his own home if at all feasible. REIT's or Real Estate Investment Trusts offer some of the advantages of owning Real Estate without the hassle, but these are controlled investments and do not have the potential equal to that of investing on your own."

"As you begin to acquire wealth, you will begin to consider diversifying your assets. Each person will have his own reasons for structuring this diversification. However, there is one basic structure that will handle all of your assets and considerations for diversifying. This structure is the Investment Pyramid.

It is structured so that the base of the pyramid is made up of your safest rock solid investments. The top of the pyramid is the area available for your most risky assets. I will draw this pyramid on the blackboard."

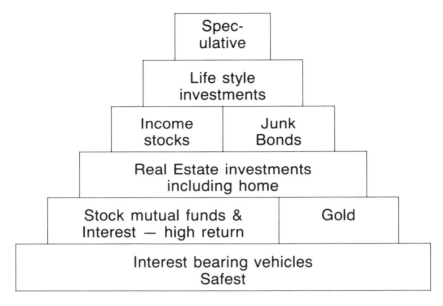

"This concept provides some diversification but keeps the majority of your assets in the safe area."

"Mr. Richmon, Why have you put gold near the bottom of the pyrammid?" said Vicky.

"Gold is the only money that will always be money regardless of anything that man may do. Gold is always the money of last resort. Wars, civilizations, governments, and politicians all may come and go, but gold will always **be** buying power instead of **representing** buying power. Gold is your hedge against any kind of change in world conditions. Although it bears no interest, it appreciates drastically as most other assets decrease. It is insurance that protects against change in economic reality."

"Now I want to draw an example of how the investment pyramid might look for someone who has acquired wealth through Real Estate."

"Notice in this case, that the safest investments, what-ever they may be should be at the bottom of the pyramid, thus being the largest investment. The quality of investments decreases as the steps of the pyramid move to the top."

Steve spoke up, "The top step must represent the portion that one does not necessarily plan to lose but could afford to lose."

"That's correct," said Mr. Richmon. "Knowing and applying this concept to your assets will go a long way toward keeping you in balance regarding risk and reward."

"There is a standard and accepted way to list your assets and your liabilities. It is called a **Financial Statement**. I will pass out a sample financial statement for you to take home and study. You will find that your own financial statement will give you a way of keeping score of your progress in acquiring wealth. It is also something that the banks will require when you want to borrow money."

"Next week will be our last session and I think you will find it quite interesting. We will discuss luck and opportunity."

"The class is dismissed."

(See Appendix II page 169 for the sample Financial Statement.)

Mr. Richmon sat on the edge if his desk and began the last session of Wealth Acquisition 101.

"Today we will discuss luck and opportunity. Let's ask the question, does luck play a part in acquiring wealth?"

Ken spoke up, "I think in some cases that it does, I know a guy who is just naturally lucky. He is always at the right place at the right time when opportunity knocks."

Aaron raised his hand, "Perhaps we should first try to define luck. Is there a definition of luck?"

Karen said, "If there is a definition for luck, wouldn't it have to include bad luck as well as good luck?"

"I can give you an example of bad luck," said David, "being struck by lightening."

"That suggests a definition," said Aaron. "Luck is something that happens to you that is not a result of anything that you did. It just happened out of the blue."

Vicky spoke up, "How about when someone wins the lottery? That's got to be the height of luck, but they had to do something, they had to pay their money and sign up."

"I give up," said Carol, "what is the definition of luck?"

Mr. Richmon smiled, "It is elusive, isn't it? Let's discuss the situation Ken described. He knows someone who just happened to be at the right place at the right time to take advantage of an opportunity. Perhaps you would like to describe the situation you have in mind."

"I can think of a lot of examples, but the first one that comes to mind is when I went with Mr. Striker to an auction. A house and all the contents were being auctioned. Mr. Striker waited until everything had been auctioned and the house and land came up. There was only one other bidder and he didn't seem to want the house that badly, so Mr. Striker bought it for a song. Less than a week later he sold the house for about 30% more than he paid for it. On top of that he borrowed the money to pay for the house from the bank on a 90 day note. His return on that deal, as we have learned to calculate it, was astronomical. He's always doing something like that...luckiest guy I ever saw!"

Mr. Richmon smiled again, "The way I see it Ken, you were just as lucky as Mr. Striker was!"

"How do you get that?" said Ken, "I didn't make any money on the deal."

"Why not?" said Mr. Richmon.

"Because I didn't have the money to buy...I think I see where you're coming from, Mr. Richmon. I had the same opportunity that Mr. Striker did. In fact, I was just as lucky as he was. Actually, it wasn't luck at all, everyone at the auction was at the right place at the right time. But, Mr. Striker was the only one who had the money and the knowledge to take advantage of the opportunity!"

"That's the way it is with most situations that people think of as luck. It wasn't luck at all. Mr. Striker made his own luck because he first put some effort and forethought in making arrangements with the bank and finding out about the auction.

Once he had purchased the house, he had the know-how to turn around and sell it for a nice profit."

"It is apparent now," said Steve, "that people make their own luck. There is a good reason that they are at the right place at the right time...because of what they have done up until that time to be able to take advantage of the situation. So it is really not luck at all, it's just what some people call luck."

David spoke up, "Now I know what my father means when he says, 'the harder you work, the luckier you get.'"

Carol raised her hand, "We know that most things which people think are luck are not luck at all. So, what is luck?"

"How about this," said Aaron, "luck is an unexpected gift out of the blue. It is a gift because you did not have to do anything or even be prepared to receive it."

"That sounds like a good definition for good luck," said Vicky, "but if our definition is to include bad luck as well as good luck, then gift is not the right word."

"Okay," said Aaron, "how about this. 'Luck is an unexpected thing that is received without qualifications.' A **thing** can be good or bad and, without qualifications, means that you did not have to do anything or be prepared to have it happen to you."

"Perhaps luck eludes an exact definition," said Mr. Richmon. "But you have certainly zeroed in on the concept. I am sure that no one in this class will ever attribute the acquisition of wealth to luck."

"That was certainly a provocative and lively discussion. Now let's talk about opportunity."

"It may seem strange at first, but when you have begun to acquire wealth, it will seem that opportunities will come your way more often than you ever expected. But when you stop and think about it, it is simply because you have the money to take advantage of the opportunity. For example, when Ken went to the auction with Mr. Striker, he did not see that as an opportunity for him, because he did not have the money to take advantage of the opportunity. But it was certainly an opportunity for Mr. Striker because he did have the money!"

"Another thing that may seem strange at first is that most opportunities **that come to you are opportunities to lose money**. The biggest problem you will have is to analyze the deal and decide on these two criteria:

[1] Is the opportunity for you?
[2] Is the opportunity sound?

"The first consideration will quickly eliminate many opportunities. **Is this opportunity for me?** First, is it in a field that I know something about? If not, pass on it. Second, could this opportunity, no matter how good it appears, put me in a make or break position. If it could, pass."

"What do you mean by 'make or break situation?'" asked Carol.

"That means, is there any way that the opportunity could put me in a position of losing what I have gained up until now? For example, remember the deal that Charlie got into with the 'big shots'? Initially, it was a good opportunity for Charlie. He put no up-front money in it so all he had in the deal was his time when the other partners decided that everyone should put up $10,000."

"That was a make of break situation for Charlie, If he put up the $10,000 he would have to sell his apartments which represented most of his wealth. Then if the deal went sour, he had lost it all. Charlie should have done one of two things; either cut his losses and run, or find some one who would be willing to buy half of Charlie's equity in the project by assuming any liabilities that might accrue to Charlie. Charlie could have sweetened the deal even more by offering to pay back the up-front money his prospective partner might put up out of their initial income from the property."

"If you can get by the first consideration, **is this deal for me**, then you must evaluate the second part which is, **is the opportunity sound**. Some of the vital questions are:

[1] Are reputable people involved?
[2] What guarantees will be given?
[3] Can you control the situation?

"One thing I have found over the years is, **my first thought is my best thought**. I have noticed that many people I know in this business have agreed with this. Another way I have heard it put is, '**Think long, think wrong**."

"Another good axiom is, '**if in doubt stay out**'. No opportunity is too good to turn down if you have reason to have doubts about it. On the other hand, you must have the nerve to act if everything adds up."

Mr. Richmon paused, sat down on the edge of his desk and looked out over the class. "I would like to wind up this last session by trying to make each of you aware of the opportunity **you** have today. Don't ever think that there is something wrong about being wealthy. If you hear someone say that 'money is the root of all evil', set him straight in a hurry. The Bible (which he is miss quoting) states, 1 Timothy Chapter 6, verse 10; For the **love** of money is the root of all evil.'"

"It is true that wealth will not bring happiness as an end in itself; however, wealth can make a valid contribution to happiness by providing the environment that allows you to do what you really want to do in the way you want to do it."

"One of the most fascinating things about acquiring wealth is that the process of acquiring it is as rewarding as the final result. There is a continuing sense of satisfaction and achievement in watching your plan work and knowing that you are controlling your own destiny."

"You will enjoy the process, and the opportunities that you can now take advantage of. You should celebrate your little successes along the way and begin to enjoy it (without adversely diminishing it) while you are still young."

"Today you have youth which is time. You have the secret to acquiring wealth. That is worth more than wealth. Wealth can be lost, and without the secret will be gone forever. **Of more value than wealth is the secret to acquiring wealth**."

"The serendipity of The Wisdom of the Ages in Acquiring Wealth is that **acquiring** wealth is more fun and more rewarding than being wealthy. Understanding this eliminates the propensity to rush the process."

"My wish is that each of you find this out for yourselves."

"Class is dismissed."

As Mr. Richmon turned and walked out of the room, the class spontaneously rose and gave him a round of applause that could be heard all the way to the football field...thus ending the final session of Wealth Acquisition 101.

THE END

EPILOGUE

When I graduated from high school many years ago, I had no concept of personal money management. My parents handled money much like the Browns. A typical middle class family that spent every dime that came in on "absolute necessities".

About five years after I graduated from college, I happened on a little book (first published in 1926) titled THE RICHEST MAN IN BABYLON by Geroge S. Clason. At that time my own family was also a typical middle class family just like the Browns. If I had missed a pay check it would have been a problem...a big problem!

That little book introduced me to the concept of paying myself first. Although this concept had certainly been around since man began to use money, I was astonished that I had never heard it...at least not in such a way that it motivated me to do it.

From the day I read that little book, my life changed. I actually did it; paid myself first, and now, more than twenty years later, by some people's standards I would be considered wealthy. But, it all started with the concept of paying yourself first.

Over the years, I have probably given away five hundred copies of that book to friends and neighbors. I have made my children read it from the time they learned to read. The RICHEST MAN IN BABYLON is a random collection of stories on the benefits of saving money. The setting is in ancient Babylon and money is gold.

For the last few years I have thought about writing a book

about my experiences (from the time I began to pay myself first) in such a way that it could be taught in high school. Gradually, the book began to take shape in my mind as a class room situation with the concepts taught in modern day parables applicable to our financially sophisticated society.

Often I reflect on the thought, "where would I be now if I had learned what is in this book, when I was a senior in high school." It is my fervent desire that somehow, some way, what is in this book will become a high school course. Our schools teach our children almost everything but what will help the most...how to manage their money and at the same time motivate them to do it.

To facilitate this, anyone has my permission and encouragement to use this book or any part of to teach the course referred in this book as Wealth Acquisition 101.

Also, if you have children or friends that would benefit from reading this book, I have included three order forms on the following page. If you order three copies the price is discounted to $15 per copy. You may use the "COMPLIMENTS OF" card or if you prefer you may write a personal note to the recipient...either way we will include it in the flyleaf of the book.

This is the deluxe edition. We are prepared to publish a less expensive paperback edition for schools if the demand develops. Let's teach this to our kids!

CAVIDA LTD.
P. O. BOX 416
McLEANSVILLE, N. C. 27301

Please send a copy of the deluxe addition of THE WISDOM
OF THE AGES IN ACQUIRING WEALTH to:

NAME _____

ADDRESS _____

CITY _____ STATE _____ ZIP _____

[ ] Enclosed is my check for $17.50 for 1 copy.
[ ] Enclosed is my check for $45.00 for 3 copies.

THIS BOOK HAS
BEEN SENT TO
YOU WITH THE
COMPLIMENTS OF

CAVIDA LTD.
P. O. BOX 416
McLEANSVILLE, N. C. 27301

Please send a copy of the deluxe addition of THE WISDOM
OF THE AGES IN ACQUIRING WEALTH to:

NAME _____

ADDRESS _____

CITY _____ STATE _____ ZIP _____

[ ] Enclosed is my check for $17.50 for 1 copy.
[ ] Enclosed is my check for $45.00 for 3 copies.

THIS BOOK HAS
BEEN SENT TO
YOU WITH THE
COMPLIMENTS OF

CAVIDA LTD.
P. O. BOX 416
McLEANSVILLE, N. C. 27301

Please send a copy of the deluxe addition of THE WISDOM
OF THE AGES IN ACQUIRING WEALTH to:

NAME _____

ADDRESS _____

CITY _____ STATE _____ ZIP _____

[ ] Enclosed is my check for $17.50 for 1 copy.
[ ] Enclosed is my check for $45.00 for 3 copies.

THIS BOOK HAS
BEEN SENT TO
YOU WITH THE
COMPLIMENTS OF

FINAL EXAM

FINAL EXAM
Sessions 1 through 15
(Answers on page 120).

There may be more than one correct answer for each question. Circle **all** correct answers.

1. Acquiring wealth requires which of the following?

   [A] Education   [D] Luck
   [B] Intelligence   [E] Know how
   [C] Hard work   [F] Sophistication

2. The secret of acquiring wealth has three parts.

1st	2nd	3rd
[A] Acquire	[B] Increase	[C] Produce
[D] Accumulate	[E] Income	[F] Protect

3. The wealth equation is:

   [A] $I = O - E$ [D] $I = A - N$
   [B] $A = I - N$ [E] $I = N - A$
   [C] $A = N - E$ [F] $A = I - E$

4. Which of the following substantiates the most popular misconception of the ages?

   [A] It takes every cent we make just to make ends meet.
   [B] If we made more money we would have enough to pay ourselves first.

5. Circle the three steps necessary to get out of the trap most people are in.

   [A] Stop buying on credit
   [B] Let the family get involved
   [C] Eliminate impulse buying
   [D] Decide what you do not need
   [E] Set up a special budget

116

6. ACCUMULATING is money earned and kept. INCREASING means making profits on money accumulated.

[A] True   [B] False

7. If you pay yourself about $4,000 per year for 30 years, to delay one year will cost you about:

[A] $4,000   [B] $50,000

8. The main reason Dr. Kevin Sawyer was able to acquire wealth in Real Estate was:

[A] He had a good reputation with his bankers.
[B] He got good advice from Bill Davis.
[C] He sought out and hired an expert to handle each stage of the development process for him.

9. Real Profit is the profit on a sum of money in excess of the profit from compound interest.

[A] True   [B] False

10. The secret to acquiring wealth in the stock market is to seek out those who have demonstrated they can make money by their track records and invest in their mutual funds.

[A] True   [B] False

11. The only kind of insurance that fits the plan for the person who wants to acquire wealth is:

[A] Ordinary Life Insurance.
[B] Term Insurance.
[C] Paid up annuity.

12. The three things we need to protect our wealth from are:

[A] Crooks   [D] Governments
[B] Other people   [E] Relatives
[C] Inflation   [F] Ourselves

13. Protecting wealth from other people falls into two of the following categories:

[A] Ethics   [D] Truth
[B] Honesty   [E] Compassion
[C] Greed   [F] Fairness

14. The great truth Mr. Richmon discovered in his dealings with Jim was:

[A] Help a friend to help himself
[B] Don't make his problems your problems
[C] Help those who can't help themselves

15. The best protection against governments regarding wealth is:

[A] Get liquid   [C] To set up options
[B] Move   [D] Buy gold

16. If the interest on $10,000 for 30 years at 4% is $22,433, what is the interest on the same at 8%?

[A] $44,866 - Twice as much
[B] $67,299 - Three times as much
[C] $90,626 - Four times as much

17. Inflation can be defined as, increasing the money supply in excess of the increase of goods and services.

[A] True   [B] False

18. Except when you go into business for yourself, you should never allow yourself to be drawn into a "make or break" situation.

[A] True   [B] False

19. You know how to acquire wealth. The two reasons you won't succeed are:

[1] You will put off paying yourself first
[2] You will not have the patience to become wealthy slowly and surely.

[A] True   [B] False

20. If money is worth 8%, how much will $5,500.00 be worth in 7 years if compounded annually?

[A] $9,369.33   [B] $9,426.03   [C] $9,505.36

21. The same problem if compounded monthly?

[A] $9,420   [B] $9,610   [C] $9,708

22. At 8% interest compounded monthly, how much money **today** will be worth $25,000 eight years from now?

[A] $13,210   [B] $15,521   [C] $14,321

23. If you pay yourself $400 per month, how much will you have in 30 years if money is worth 8% compounded annually?

[A] $550,467   [B] $533,259   [C] $543,759

24. If you want to accumulate $650,000 in 32 years, how much must you pay yourself per month at 8% interest compounded yearly?

[A] $476.92   [B] $403.58   [C] $510.23

ANSWERS TO QUIZZES

QUIZ #1	QUIZ #2	QUIZ #3	QUIZ #4
1. [E]	1. [D]	1. [A]	1. [B]
2. [B]	[B]	2. [A]	[D]
3. [D]	[F]	3. [A]	2. [A]
[B]	2. [A]	4. [C]	[D]
[F]	3. [B]	5. [C]	3. [B]
4. [A]	4. [A]	6. [A]	4. [B]
[C]	[B]	7. [C]	5. [C]
[E]	[C]	8. [A]	6. [C]
5. [B]	5. [B]	9. [B]	7. [E]
6. [B]	6. [E]	10. [C]	8. [E]
7. [A]	7. [A]		9. [A]
[B]	8. [A]		10. [A]
8. [A]	9. [C]		
[C]	10. [C]		
[E]			
9. [C]			
10. [A]			
[B]			
[C]			

ANSWERS TO FINAL EXAM

1. [E]	7. [B]	13. [C]	19. [A]
2. [D]	8. [C]	[E]	20. [B]
[B]	9. [A]	14. [B]	21. [B]
[F]	10. [A]	15. [C]	22. [A]
3. [B]	11. [B]	16. [C]	23. [C]
4. [A]	12. [B]	17. [A]	24. [B]
[B]	[D]	18. [A]	
5. [A]	[F]		
[C]			
[E]			
6. [A]			

APPENDIX I

COMPOUND INTEREST PROBLEMS

AND

INTEREST TABLES

COMPOUND INTEREST

To understand compound interest, let's first discuss simple interest.

PROBLEM: Find the amount of simple interest earned on $1,000 for 5 years at 8%.

I = The amount of Interest earned.
P = Principal (The amount drawing interest.)
R = Rate (The interest rate per period.)
T = Time

The equation for simple interest is

I = PRT (Principal times Rate times Time.)

Substituting in the equation we have:

I = $1,000 x .08 x 5
I = $ 400

The total amount of money at the end of 5 years would be:

P + I (Principal plus Interest.)

Total = $1,000 + 400 = $1,400

Simple enough so far...Now we will discuss compound interest.

Compound interest means calculating the interest at the end of a specified period of time and adding that interest to the principal so that for the next period we will be earning interest on both the principal and interest of the previous period.

The PERIOD can be whatever we want it to be. Usually the period is a year or a month. In our calculations, we will use either a year or a month for the PERIOD.

Now we will work the same problem except this time we will use the concept of COMPOUND interest. The PERIOD will be one year. Therefore, we will calculate the interest for the first year and add it to the PRINCIPAL and then use that amount as the PRINCIPAL for the next year.

I = PRT
I = $1,000.00 x .08 x 1 ⎫ Amount of interest
I = $80   ⎬ for the **first** PERIOD
                          ⎭ which is 1 year.

Total PRINCIPAL = $1,000.00 + 80.00 = $1,080.00

I = PRT
I = $1,080.00 x .08 x 1 ⎫ Amount of interest
I = $86.40   ⎬ for the **second** PERIOD
                          ⎭ which is 1 year.

Total PRINCIPAL = $1,080.00 + 86.40 = $1,166.40

I = PRT
I = $1,166.40 x .08 x 1 ⎫ Amount of interest
I = $93.31   ⎬ for the **third** PERIOD
                          ⎭ which is 1 year.

Total PRINCIPAL = $1,166.40 + 93.31 = $1,259.71

I = PRT
I = $1,259.71 x .08 x 1 ⎫ Amount of interest
I = $100.78   ⎬ for the **fourth** PERIOD
                          ⎭ which is 1 year.

Total PRINCIPAL = $1,259.71 + 100.78 = $1,360.49

I = PRT
I = $1,360.49 x .08 x 1 ⎤— Amount of interest
I = $108.84   ⎦   for the **fifth** PERIOD.
                             which is 1 year.

Total PRINCIPAL = $1,360.49 + 108.84 = $1,469.33

That is how compound interest works. For the five year period, compound interest produced $69.33 more return than simple interest. That may not seem like much difference for five years, but remember that the compound interest curve increases geometrically. (Refer to the compound interest curve on page 24.)

Fortunately, there is a much faster way to calculate compound interest. It is by using interest tables. The interest tables to use for compound interest are **TABLE 1** titled **AMOUNT OF 1**. These tables are immediately following this discussion beginning on page 128.

Now let's see how simple it is to solve the above problem with tables. We will use the equation $S = AC$ where A = $1,000, the present value and C = a **constant** found in the tables.

[1] Determine the interest rate PER PERIOD. In this case the PERIOD is one year and the interest rate is 8% PER YEAR.
[2] Turn to the tables and locate the column titled 8%. (page 135.)
[3] The column titled n stands for number of PERIODS. Move down to the number 1.4693 2808. This is the **constant**, the value of **one dollar** compounded at 8% for 5

periods... thus the title of the chart **How $1 deposited at Compound Interest will grow.**

[4] Multiplying the **constant** by $1,000.00 gives The **future value** of $1,469.33 rounded off to two decimal places.

That's all there is to it when the period is in years. However, if the PERIOD is not in years, there is one catch...**the interest rate must be converted from the yearly interest rate to the PERIOD interest rate**.

To convert the yearly or annual interest rate to the PERIOD interest rate simply divide the annual rate by the number of periods in a year. For example, to find the **monthly** interest rate if the annual rate is 8%, divide 8 by 12 which equals 2/3 or 2/3%. This is the interest rate to use to calculate compound interest which is compounded monthly.

Now, let's find out how much $1,000 will be worth in 5 years **compounded monthly**. We will follow the same four step procedure as before. The equation is $S = AC$ where A = $1,000 and C is the **constant** from the tables.

[1] Determine the interest rate PER PERIOD.
   In this case the PERIOD is one month. Divide the interest rate by 12 and obtain 2/3%.
[2] Turn to the table and locate the column titled 2/3%. (Page 129.)
[3] The column titled n stands for number of PERIODS. Move down to the number 60 (5 years x 12 periods) and under 2/3% you will see the constant 1.4898 4571.
[4] Multiplying the **constant** by $1,000.00 gives the future value of $1,489.85 rounded off to two decimal places.

The difference between compounding yearly and compounding monthly is $20.52. That difference may not

125

seem significant, however, in Mr. White's 30 year plan that difference was $41,873.52.

The tables presented here only go up to 150 periods for the smaller rates and to 50 periods for the highest rates. A complete set of tables would take over 700 pages to present.

For those who want to be able to calculate any rate for any time period, I would recommend the following book:

FINANCIAL COMPOUND INTEREST AND ANNUITY TABLES
Fifth Edition
Publication No. 376
Financial Publishing Company
BOSTON

For an in depth study of Compound interest, annuities, sinking funds and related mathematics, I would recommend the following book:

Schaum's Outline Series
Theory and problems of
MATHEMATICS OF FINANCE
By Frank Ayres, Jr.
McGraw-Hill Book Company
New York, St. Louis, San Francisco, Toronto, Sydney

This book contains over 500 solved problems. Both books can usually be found at a college or university book store.

This completes the solution for our first category of interest problems which is FUTURE VALUE OF A PRESENT AMOUNT OF MONEY which was discussed in Session 9 page 62.

The very important concept of REAL PROFIT utilizes what we have learned here. Real Profit is profit in excess of that produced by compound interest as set out above.

Now turn to page 136 for a discussion of the second category, PRESENT VALUE OF A FUTURE VALUE OF MONEY.

TABLE I - AMOUNT OF 1
How $1 deposited at compound interest will grow

n	$\frac{1}{4}\%$	$\frac{1}{3}\%$	$\frac{5}{12}\%$	$\frac{1}{2}\%$	$\frac{7}{12}\%$	$\frac{2}{3}\%$	n
1	1.0025 0000	1.0033 3333	1.0041 6667	1.0050 0000	1.0058 3333	1.0066 6667	1
2	1.0050 0625	1.0066 7778	1.0083 5069	1.0100 2500	1.0117 0069	1.0133 7778	2
3	1.0075 1877	1.0100 3337	1.0125 5216	1.0150 7513	1.0176 0228	1.0201 3363	3
4	1.0100 3756	1.0134 0015	1.0167 7112	1.0201 5050	1.0235 3830	1.0269 3452	4
5	1.0125 6266	1.0167 7815	1.0210 0767	1.0252 5125	1.0295 0894	1.0337 8075	5
6	1.0150 9406	1.0201 6741	1.0252 6187	1.0303 7751	1.0355 1440	1.0406 7262	6
7	1.0176 3180	1.0235 6797	1.0295 3379	1.0355 2940	1.0415 5490	1.0476 1044	7
8	1.0201 7588	1.0269 7986	1.0338 2352	1.0407 0704	1.0476 3064	1.0545 9451	8
9	1.0227 2632	1.0304 0313	1.0381 3111	1.0459 1058	1.0537 4182	1.0616 2514	9
10	1.0252 8313	1.0338 3780	1.0424 5666	1.0511 4013	1.0598 8865	1.0687 0264	10
11	1.0278 4634	1.0372 8393	1.0468 0023	1.0563 9583	1.0660 7133	1.0758 2732	11
12	1.0304 1596	1.0407 4154	1.0511 6190	1.0616 7781	1.0722 9008	1.0829 9951	12
13	1.0329 9200	1.0442 1068	1.0555 4174	1.0669 8620	1.0785 4511	1.0902 1950	13
14	1.0355 7448	1.0476 9138	1.0599 3983	1.0723 2113	1.0848 3662	1.0974 8763	14
15	1.0381 6341	1.0511 8369	1.0643 5625	1.0776 8274	1.0911 6483	1.1048 0422	15
16	1.0407 5882	1.0546 8763	1.0687 9106	1.0830 7115	1.0975 2996	1.1121 6958	16
17	1.0433 6072	1.0582 0326	1.0732 4436	1.0884 8651	1.1039 3222	1.1195 8404	17
18	1.0459 6912	1.0617 3060	1.0777 1621	1.0939 2894	1.1103 7182	1.1270 4794	18
19	1.0485 8404	1.0652 6971	1.0822 0670	1.0993 9858	1.1168 4899	1.1345 6159	19
20	1.0512 0550	1.0688 2060	1.0867 1589	1.1048 9558	1.1233 6395	1.1421 2533	20
21	1.0538 3352	1.0723 8334	1.0912 4387	1.1104 2006	1.1299 1690	1.1497 3950	21
22	1.0564 6810	1.0759 5795	1.0957 9072	1.1159 7216	1.1365 0808	1.1574 0443	22
23	1.0591 0927	1.0795 4448	1.1003 5652	1.1215 5202	1.1431 3771	1.1651 2046	23
24	1.0617 5704	1.0831 4296	1.1049 4134	1.1271 5978	1.1498 0602	1.1728 8793	24
25	1.0644 1144	1.0867 5344	1.1095 4526	1.1327 9558	1.1565 1322	1.1807 0718	25
26	1.0670 7247	1.0903 7595	1.1141 6836	1.1384 5955	1.1632 5955	1.1885 7857	26
27	1.0697 4015	1.0940 1053	1.1188 1073	1.1441 5185	1.1700 4523	1.1965 0242	27
28	1.0724 1450	1.0976 5724	1.1234 7244	1.1498 7261	1.1768 7049	1.2044 7911	28
29	1.0750 9553	1.1013 1609	1.1281 5358	1.1556 2197	1.1837 3557	1.2125 0897	29
30	1.0777 8327	1.1049 8715	1.1328 5422	1.1614 0008	1.1906 4069	1.2205 9236	30
31	1.0804 7773	1.1086 7044	1.1375 7444	1.1672 0708	1.1975 8610	1.2287 2964	31
32	1.0831 7892	1.1123 6601	1.1423 1434	1.1730 4312	1.2045 7202	1.2369 2117	32
33	1.0858 8687	1.1160 7389	1.1470 7398	1.1789 0833	1.2115 9869	1.2451 6731	33
34	1.0886 0159	1.1197 9414	1.1518 5346	1.1848 0288	1.2186 6634	1.2534 6843	34
35	1.0913 2309	1.1235 2679	1.1566 5284	1.1907 2689	1.2257 7523	1.2618 2489	35
36	1.0940 5140	1.1272 7187	1.1614 7223	1.1966 8052	1.2329 2559	1.2702 3705	36
37	1.0967 8653	1.1310 2945	1.1663 1170	1.2026 6393	1.2401 1765	1.2787 0530	37
38	1.0995 2850	1.1347 9955	1.1711 7133	1.2086 7725	1.2473 5167	1.2872 3000	38
39	1.1022 7732	1.1385 8221	1.1760 5121	1.2147 2063	1.2546 2789	1.2958 1153	39
40	1.1050 3301	1.1423 7748	1.1809 5142	1.2207 9424	1.2619 4655	1.3044 5028	40
41	1.1077 9559	1.1461 8541	1.1858 7206	1.2268 9821	1.2693 0791	1.3131 4661	41
42	1.1105 6508	1.1500 0603	1.1908 1319	1.2330 3270	1.2767 1220	1.3219 0092	42
43	1.1133 4149	1.1538 3938	1.1957 7491	1.2391 9786	1.2841 5969	1.3307 1360	43
44	1.1161 2485	1.1576 8551	1.2007 5731	1.2453 9385	1.2916 5062	1.3395 8502	44
45	1.1189 1516	1.1615 4446	1.2057 6046	1.2516 2082	1.2991 8525	1.3485 1559	45
46	1.1217 1245	1.1654 1628	1.2107 8446	1.2578 7892	1.3067 6383	1.3575 0569	46
47	1.1245 1673	1.1693 0100	1.2158 2940	1.2641 6832	1.3143 8662	1.3665 5573	47
48	1.1273 2802	1.1731 9867	1.2208 9536	1.2704 8916	1.3220 5388	1.3756 6610	48
49	1.1301 4634	1.1771 0933	1.2259 8242	1.2768 4161	1.3297 6586	1.3848 3721	49
50	1.1329 7171	1.1810 3303	1.2310 9068	1.2832 2581	1.3375 2283	1.3940 6946	50

TABLE I - AMOUNT OF 1
How $1 deposited at compound interest will grow

n	$\frac{1}{4}\%$	$\frac{1}{3}\%$	$\frac{5}{12}\%$	$\frac{1}{2}\%$	$\frac{7}{12}\%$	$\frac{2}{3}\%$	n
51	1.1358 0414	1.1849 6981	1.2362 2022	1.2896 4194	1.3453 2504	1.4033 6325	51
52	1.1386 4365	1.1889 1971	1.2413 7114	1.2960 9015	1.3531 7277	1.4127 1901	52
53	1.1414 9026	1.1928 8277	1.2465 4352	1.3025 7060	1.3610 6628	1.4221 3713	53
54	1.1443 4398	1.1968 5905	1.2517 3745	1.3090 8346	1.3690 0583	1.4316 1805	54
55	1.1472 0484	1.2008 4858	1.2569 5302	1.3156 2887	1.3769 9170	1.4411 6217	55
56	1.1500 7285	1.2048 5141	1.2621 9033	1.3222 0702	1.3850 2415	1.4507 6992	56
57	1.1529 4804	1.2088 6758	1.2674 4946	1.3288 1805	1.3931 0346	1.4604 4172	57
58	1.1558 3041	1.2128 9714	1.2727 3050	1.3354 6214	1.4012 2990	1.4701 7799	58
59	1.1587 1998	1.2169 4013	1.2780 3354	1.3421 3946	1.4094 0374	1.4799 7918	59
60	1.1616 1678	1.2209 9659	1.2833 5868	1.3488 5015	1.4176 2526	1.4898 4571	60
61	1.1645 2082	1.2250 6658	1.2887 0601	1.3555 9440	1.4258 9474	1.4997 7801	61
62	1.1674 3213	1.2291 5014	1.2940 7561	1.3623 7238	1.4342 1246	1.5097 7653	62
63	1.1703 5071	1.2332 4730	1.2994 6760	1.3691 8424	1.4425 7870	1.5198 4171	63
64	1.1732 7658	1.2373 5813	1.3048 8204	1.3760 3016	1.4509 9374	1.5299 7399	64
65	1.1762 0977	1.2414 8266	1.3103 1905	1.3829 1031	1.4594 5787	1.5401 7381	65
66	1.1791 5030	1.2456 2093	1.3157 7872	1.3898 2486	1.4679 7138	1.5504 4164	66
67	1.1820 9817	1.2497 7300	1.3212 6113	1.3967 7399	1.4765 3454	1.5607 7792	67
68	1.1850 5342	1.2539 3891	1.3267 6638	1.4037 5785	1.4851 4766	1.5711 8310	68
69	1.1880 1605	1.2581 1871	1.3322 9458	1.4107 7664	1.4938 1102	1.5816 5766	69
70	1.1909 8609	1.2623 1244	1.3378 4580	1.4178 3053	1.5025 2492	1.5922 0204	70
71	1.1939 6356	1.2665 2015	1.3434 2016	1.4249 1968	1.5112 8965	1.6028 1672	71
72	1.1969 4847	1.2707 4188	1.3490 1774	1.4320 4428	1.5201 0550	1.6135 0217	72
73	1.1999 4084	1.2749 7769	1.3546 3865	1.4392 0450	1.5289 7279	1.6242 5885	73
74	1.2029 4069	1.2792 2761	1.3602 8298	1.4464 0052	1.5378 9179	1.6350 8724	74
75	1.2059 4804	1.2834 9170	1.3659 5082	1.4536 3252	1.5468 6283	1.6459 8782	75
76	1.2089 6291	1.2877 7001	1.3716 4229	1.4609 0069	1.5558 8620	1.6569 6107	76
77	1.2119 8532	1.2920 6258	1.3773 5746	1.4682 0519	1.5649 6220	1.6680 0748	77
78	1.2150 1528	1.2963 6945	1.3830 9645	1.4755 4622	1.5740 9115	1.6791 2753	78
79	1.2180 5282	1.3006 9068	1.3888 5935	1.4829 2395	1.5832 7334	1.6903 2172	79
80	1.2210 9795	1.3050 2632	1.3946 4627	1.4903 3857	1.5925 0910	1.7015 9053	80
81	1.2241 5070	1.3093 7641	1.4004 5729	1.4977 9026	1.6017 9874	1.7129 3446	81
82	1.2272 1108	1.3137 4099	1.4062 9253	1.5052 7921	1.6111 4257	1.7243 5403	82
83	1.2302 7910	1.3181 2013	1.4121 5209	1.5128 0561	1.6205 4090	1.7358 4972	83
84	1.2333 5480	1.3225 1386	1.4180 3605	1.5203 6964	1.6299 9405	1.7474 2205	84
85	1.2364 3819	1.3269 2224	1.4239 4454	1.5279 7148	1.6395 0235	1.7590 7153	85
86	1.2395 2928	1.3313 4532	1.4298 7764	1.5356 1134	1.6490 6612	1.7707 9868	86
87	1.2426 2811	1.3357 8314	1.4358 3546	1.5432 8940	1.6586 8567	1.7826 0400	87
88	1.2457 3468	1.3402 3575	1.4418 1811	1.5510 0585	1.6683 6134	1.7944 8003	88
89	1.2488 4901	1.3447 0320	1.4478 2568	1.5587 6087	1.6780 9344	1.8064 5128	89
90	1.2519 7114	1.3491 8554	1.4538 5829	1.5665 5468	1.6878 8232	1.8184 9429	90
91	1.2551 0106	1.3536 8283	1.4599 1603	1.5743 8745	1.6977 2830	1.8306 1758	91
92	1.2582 3882	1.3581 9510	1.4659 9902	1.5822 5939	1.7076 3172	1.8428 2170	92
93	1.2613 8441	1.3627 2242	1.4721 0735	1.5901 7069	1.7175 9290	1.8551 0718	93
94	1.2645 3787	1.3672 6483	1.4782 4113	1.5981 2154	1.7276 1219	1.8674 7456	94
95	1.2676 9922	1.3718 2238	1.4844 0047	1.6061 1215	1.7376 8993	1.8799 2439	95
96	1.2708 6847	1.3763 9512	1.4905 8547	1.6141 4271	1.7478 2646	1.8924 5722	96
97	1.2740 4564	1.3809 8310	1.4967 9624	1.6222 1342	1.7580 2211	1.9050 7360	97
98	1.2772 3075	1.3855 8638	1.5030 3289	1.6303 2449	1.7682 7724	1.9177 7409	98
99	1.2804 2383	1.3902 0500	1.5092 9553	1.6384 7611	1.7785 9219	1.9305 5925	99
100	1.2836 2489	1.3948 3902	1.5155 8426	1.6466 6849	1.7889 6731	1.9434 2965	100

TABLE I - AMOUNT OF 1
How $1 deposited at compound interest will grow

n	$\frac{1}{3}\%$	$\frac{3}{8}\%$	$\frac{5}{12}\%$	$\frac{1}{2}\%$	$\frac{7}{12}\%$	$\frac{2}{3}\%$	n
101	1.2868 3395	1.3994 8848	1.5218 9919	1.6549 0183	1.7994 0295	1.9563 8585	101
102	1.2900 5104	1.4041 5344	1.5282 4044	1.6631 7634	1.8098 9947	1.9694 2842	102
103	1.2932 7616	1.4088 3395	1.5346 0811	1.6714 9223	1.8204 5722	1.9825 5794	103
104	1.2965 0935	1.4135 3007	1.5410 0231	1.6798 4969	1.8310 7655	1.9957 7499	104
105	1.2997 5063	1.4182 4183	1.5474 2315	1.6882 4894	1.8417 5783	2.0090 8016	105
106	1.3030 0000	1.4229 6931	1.5538 7075	1.6966 9018	1.8525 0142	2.0224 7403	106
107	1.3062 5750	1.4277 1254	1.5603 4521	1.7051 7363	1.8633 0768	2.0359 5719	107
108	1.3095 2315	1.4324 7158	1.5668 4665	1.7136 9950	1.8741 7697	2.0495 3024	108
109	1.3127 9696	1.4372 4649	1.5733 7518	1.7222 6800	1.8851 0967	2.0631 9377	109
110	1.3160 7895	1.4420 3731	1.5799 3091	1.7308 7934	1.8961 0614	2.0769 4840	110
111	1.3193 6915	1.4468 4410	1.5865 1395	1.7395 3373	1.9071 6676	2.0907 9472	111
112	1.3226 6757	1.4516 6691	1.5931 2443	1.7482 3140	1.9182 9190	2.1047 3335	112
113	1.3259 7424	1.4565 0580	1.5997 6245	1.7569 7256	1.9294 8194	2.1187 6491	113
114	1.3292 8917	1.4613 6082	1.6064 2812	1.7657 5742	1.9407 3725	2.1328 9000	114
115	1.3326 1240	1.4662 3202	1.6131 2157	1.7745 8621	1.9520 5822	2.1471 0927	115
116	1.3359 4393	1.4711 1946	1.6198 4291	1.7834 5914	1.9634 4522	2.1614 2333	116
117	1.3392 8379	1.4760 2320	1.6265 9226	1.7923 7644	1.9748 9865	2.1758 3282	117
118	1.3426 3200	1.4809 4327	1.6333 6973	1.8013 3832	1.9864 1890	2.1903 3837	118
119	1.3459 8858	1.4858 7975	1.6401 7543	1.8103 4501	1.9980 0634	2.2049 4063	119
120	1.3493 5355	1.4908 3268	1.6470 0950	1.8193 9673	2.0096 6138	2.2196 4023	120
121	1.3527 2693	1.4958 0212	1.6538 7204	1.8284 9372	2.0213 8440	2.2344 3784	121
122	1.3561 0875	1.5007 8813	1.6607 6317	1.8376 3619	2.0331 7581	2.2493 3409	122
123	1.3594 9902	1.5057 9076	1.6676 8302	1.8468 2437	2.0450 3600	2.2643 2965	123
124	1.3628 9777	1.5108 1006	1.6746 3170	1.8560 5849	2.0569 6538	2.2794 2518	124
125	1.3663 0501	1.5158 4609	1.6816 0933	1.8653 3878	2.0689 6434	2.2946 2135	125
126	1.3697 2077	1.5208 9892	1.6886 1603	1.8746 6548	2.0810 3330	2.3099 1882	126
127	1.3731 4508	1.5259 6858	1.6956 5193	1.8840 3880	2.0931 7266	2.3253 1828	127
128	1.3765 7794	1.5310 5514	1.7027 1715	1.8934 5900	2.1053 8284	2.3408 2040	128
129	1.3800 1938	1.5361 5866	1.7098 1181	1.9029 2629	2.1176 6424	2.3564 2587	129
130	1.3834 6943	1.5412 7919	1.7169 3602	1.9124 4092	2.1300 1728	2.3721 3538	130
131	1.3869 2811	1.5464 1678	1.7240 8992	1.9220 0313	2.1424 4238	2.3879 4962	131
132	1.3903 9543	1.5515 7151	1.7312 7363	1.9316 1314	2.1549 3996	2.4038 6928	132
133	1.3938 7142	1.5567 4341	1.7384 8727	1.9412 7121	2.1675 1044	2.4198 9507	133
134	1.3973 5609	1.5619 3256	1.7457 3097	1.9509 7757	2.1801 5425	2.4360 2771	134
135	1.4008 4948	1.5671 3900	1.7530 0485	1.9607 3245	2.1928 7182	2.4522 6789	135
136	1.4043 5161	1.5723 6279	1.7603 0903	1.9705 3612	2.2056 6357	2.4686 1635	136
137	1.4078 6249	1.5776 0400	1.7676 4365	1.9803 8880	2.2185 2994	2.4850 7379	137
138	1.4113 8214	1.5828 6268	1.7750 0884	1.9902 9074	2.2314 7137	2.5016 4095	138
139	1.4149 1060	1.5881 3889	1.7824 0471	2.0002 4219	2.2444 8828	2.5183 1855	139
140	1.4184 4787	1.5934 3269	1.7898 3139	2.0102 4340	2.2575 8113	2.5351 0734	140
141	1.4219 9399	1.5987 4413	1.7972 8902	2.0202 9462	2.2707 5036	2.5520 0806	141
142	1.4255 4898	1.6040 7328	1.8047 7773	2.0303 9609	2.2839 9640	2.5690 2145	142
143	1.4291 1285	1.6094 2019	1.8122 9763	2.0405 4808	2.2973 1971	2.5861 4826	143
144	1.4326 8563	1.6147 8492	1.8198 4887	2.0507 5082	2.3107 2074	2.6033 8924	144
145	1.4362 6735	1.6201 6754	1.8274 3158	2.0610 0457	2.3241 9995	2.6207 4517	145
146	1.4398 5802	1.6255 6810	1.8350 4588	2.0713 0959	2.3377 5778	2.6382 1681	146
147	1.4434 5766	1.6309 8666	1.8426 9190	2.0816 6614	2.3513 9470	2.6558 0492	147
148	1.4470 6631	1.6364 2328	1.8503 6978	2.0920 7447	2.3651 1117	2.6735 1028	148
149	1.4506 8397	1.6418 7802	1.8580 7966	2.1025 3484	2.3789 0765	2.6913 3369	149
150	1.4543 1068	1.6473 5095	1.8658 2166	2.1130 4752	2.3927 8461	2.7092 7591	150

TABLE I - AMOUNT OF 1
How $1 deposited at compound interest will grow

n	$\frac{3}{4}\%$	1%	$1\frac{1}{4}\%$	$1\frac{1}{2}\%$	$1\frac{3}{4}\%$	2%	n
1	1.0075 0000	1.0100 0000	1.0125 0000	1.0150 0000	1.0175 0000	1.0200 0000	1
2	1.0150 5625	1.0201 0000	1.0251 5625	1.0302 2500	1.0353 0625	1.0404 0000	2
3	1.0226 6917	1.0303 0100	1.0379 7070	1.0456 7838	1.0534 2411	1.0612 0800	3
4	1.0303 3919	1.0406 0401	1.0509 4534	1.0613 6355	1.0718 5903	1.0824 3216	4
5	1.0380 6673	1.0510 1005	1.0640 8215	1.0772 8400	1.0906 1656	1.1040 8080	5
6	1.0458 5224	1.0615 2015	1.0773 8318	1.0934 4326	1.1097 0235	1.1261 6242	6
7	1.0536 9613	1.0721 3535	1.0908 5047	1.1098 4491	1.1291 2215	1.1486 8567	7
8	1.0615 9885	1.0828 5671	1.1044 8610	1.1264 9259	1.1488 8178	1.1716 5938	8
9	1.0695 6084	1.0936 8527	1.1182 9218	1.1433 8998	1.1689 8721	1.1950 9257	9
10	1.0775 8255	1.1046 2213	1.1322 7083	1.1605 4083	1.1894 4449	1.2189 9442	10
11	1.0856 6441	1.1156 6835	1.1464 2422	1.1779 4894	1.2102 5977	1.2433 7431	11
12	1.0938 0690	1.1268 2503	1.1607 5452	1.1956 1817	1.2314 3931	1.2682 4179	12
13	1.1020 1045	1.1380 9328	1.1752 6395	1.2135 5244	1.2529 8950	1.2936 0663	13
14	1.1102 7553	1.1494 7421	1.1899 5475	1.2317 5573	1.2749 1682	1.3194 7876	14
15	1.1186 0259	1.1609 6896	1.2048 2918	1.2502 3207	1.2972 2786	1.3458 6834	15
16	1.1269 9211	1.1725 7864	1.2198 8955	1.2689 8555	1.3199 2935	1.3727 8571	16
17	1.1354 4455	1.1843 0443	1.2351 3817	1.2880 2033	1.3430 2811	1.4002 4142	17
18	1.1439 6039	1.1961 4748	1.2505 7739	1.3073 4064	1.3665 3111	1.4282 4625	18
19	1.1525 4009	1.2081 0895	1.2662 0961	1.3269 5075	1.3904 4540	1.4568 1117	19
20	1.1611 8414	1.2201 9004	1.2820 3723	1.3468 5501	1.4147 7820	1.4859 4740	20
21	1.1698 9302	1.2323 9194	1.2980 6270	1.3670 5783	1.4395 3681	1.5156 6634	21
22	1.1786 6722	1.2447 1586	1.3142 8848	1.3875 6370	1.4647 2871	1.5459 7967	22
23	1.1875 0723	1.2571 6302	1.3307 1709	1.4083 7715	1.4903 6146	1.5768 9926	23
24	1.1964 1353	1.2697 3465	1.3473 5105	1.4295 0281	1.5164 4279	1.6084 3725	24
25	1.2053 8663	1.2824 3200	1.3641 9294	1.4509 4535	1.5429 8054	1.6406 0599	25
26	1.2144 2703	1.2952 5631	1.3812 4535	1.4727 0953	1.5699 8269	1.6734 1811	26
27	1.2235 3523	1.3082 0888	1.3985 1092	1.4948 0018	1.5974 5739	1.7068 8648	27
28	1.2327 1175	1.3212 9097	1.4159 9230	1.5172 2218	1.6254 1290	1.7410 2421	28
29	1.2419 5709	1.3345 0388	1.4336 9221	1.5399 8051	1.6538 5762	1.7758 4469	29
30	1.2512 7176	1.3478 4892	1.4516 1336	1.5630 8022	1.6828 0013	1.8113 6158	30
31	1.2606 5630	1.3613 2740	1.4697 5853	1.5865 2642	1.7122 4913	1.8475 8882	31
32	1.2701 1122	1.3749 4068	1.4881 3051	1.6103 2432	1.7422 1349	1.8845 4059	32
33	1.2796 3706	1.3886 9009	1.5067 3214	1.6344 7918	1.7727 0223	1.9222 3140	33
34	1.2892 3434	1.4025 7699	1.5255 6629	1.6589 9637	1.8037 2452	1.9606 7603	34
35	1.2989 0359	1.4166 0276	1.5446 3587	1.6838 8132	1.8352 8970	1.9998 8955	35
36	1.3086 4537	1.4307 6878	1.5639 4382	1.7091 3954	1.8674 0727	2.0398 8734	36
37	1.3184 6021	1.4450 7647	1.5834 9312	1.7347 7663	1.9000 8689	2.0806 8509	37
38	1.3283 4866	1.4595 2724	1.6032 8678	1.7607 9828	1.9333 3841	2.1222 9879	38
39	1.3383 1128	1.4741 2251	1.6233 2787	1.7872 1025	1.9671 7184	2.1647 4477	39
40	1.3483 4861	1.4888 6373	1.6436 1946	1.8140 1841	2.0015 9734	2.2080 3966	40
41	1.3584 6123	1.5037 5237	1.6641 6471	1.8412 2868	2.0366 2530	2.2522 0046	41
42	1.3686 4969	1.5187 8989	1.6849 6677	1.8688 4712	2.0722 6624	2.2972 4447	42
43	1.3789 1456	1.5339 7779	1.7060 2885	1.8968 7982	2.1085 3090	2.3431 8936	43
44	1.3892 5642	1.5493 1757	1.7273 5421	1.9253 3302	2.1454 3019	2.3900 5314	44
45	1.3996 7584	1.5648 1075	1.7489 4614	1.9542 1301	2.1829 7522	2.4378 5421	45
46	1.4101 7341	1.5804 5885	1.7708 0797	1.9835 2621	2.2211 7728	2.4866 1129	46
47	1.4207 4971	1.5962 6344	1.7929 4306	2.0132 7910	2.2600 4789	2.5363 4351	47
48	1.4314 0533	1.6122 2608	1.8153 5485	2.0434 7829	2.2995 9872	2.5870 7039	48
49	1.4421 4087	1.6283 4834	1.8380 4679	2.0741 3046	2.3398 4170	2.6388 1179	49
50	1.4529 5693	1.6446 3182	1.8610 2237	2.1052 4242	2.3807 8893	2.6915 8803	50

TABLE I - AMOUNT OF 1
How $1 deposited at compound interest will grow

n	$\frac{3}{4}\%$	1%	$1\frac{1}{4}\%$	$1\frac{1}{2}\%$	$1\frac{3}{4}\%$	2%	n
51	1.4638 5411	1.6610 7814	1.8842 8515	2.1368 2106	2.4224 5274	2.7454 1979	51
52	1.4748 3301	1.6776 8892	1.9078 3872	2.1688 7337	2.4648 4566	2.8003 2819	52
53	1.4858 9426	1.6944 6581	1.9316 8670	2.2014 0647	2.5079 8046	2.8563 3475	53
54	1.4970 3847	1.7114 1047	1.9558 3279	2.2344 2757	2.5518 7012	2.9134 6144	54
55	1.5082 6626	1.7285 2457	1.9802 8070	2.2679 4398	2.5965 2785	2.9717 3067	55
56	1.5195 7825	1.7458 0982	2.0050 3420	2.3019 6314	2.6419 6708	3.0311 6529	56
57	1.5309 7509	1.7632 6792	2.0300 9713	2.3364 9259	2.6882 0151	3.0917 8859	57
58	1.5424 5740	1.7809 0060	2.0554 7335	2.3715 3998	2.7352 4503	3.1536 2436	58
59	1.5540 2583	1.7987 0960	2.0811 6676	2.4071 1308	2.7831 1182	3.2166 9685	59
60	1.5656 8103	1.8166 9670	2.1071 8135	2.4432 1978	2.8318 1628	3.2810 3079	60
61	1.5774 2363	1.8348 6367	2.1335 2111	2.4798 6807	2.8813 7306	3.3466 5140	61
62	1.5892 5431	1.8532 1230	2.1601 9013	2.5170 6609	2.9317 9709	3.4135 8443	62
63	1.6011 7372	1.8717 4443	2.1871 9250	2.5548 2208	2.9831 0354	3.4818 5612	63
64	1.6131 8252	1.8904 6187	2.2145 3241	2.5931 4442	3.0343 0785	3.5514 9324	64
65	1.6252 8139	1.9093 6649	2.2422 1407	2.6320 4158	3.0884 2574	3.6225 2311	65
66	1.6374 7100	1.9284 6015	2.2702 4174	2.6715 2221	3.1424 7319	3.6949 7357	66
67	1.6497 5203	1.9477 4475	2.2986 1976	2.7115 9504	3.1974 6647	3.7688 7304	67
68	1.6621 2517	1.9672 2220	2.3273 5251	2.7522 6896	3.2534 2213	3.8442 5050	68
69	1.6745 9111	1.9868 9442	2.3564 4442	2.7935 5300	3.3103 5702	3.9211 3551	69
70	1.6871 5055	2.0067 6337	2.3858 9997	2.8354 5629	3.3682 8827	3.9995 5822	70
71	1.6998 0418	2.0268 3100	2.4157 2372	2.8779 8814	3.4272 3331	4.0795 4939	71
72	1.7125 5271	2.0470 9931	2.4459 2027	2.9211 5796	3.4872 0990	4.1611 4038	72
73	1.7253 9685	2.0675 7031	2.4764 9427	2.9649 7533	3.5482 3607	4.2443 6318	73
74	1.7383 3733	2.0882 4601	2.5074 5045	3.0094 4996	3.6103 3020	4.3292 5045	74
75	1.7513 7486	2.1091 2847	2.5387 9358	3.0545 9171	3.6735 1098	4.4158 3546	75
76	1.7645 1017	2.1302 1975	2.5705 2850	3.1004 1059	3.7377 9742	4.5041 5216	76
77	1.7777 4400	2.1515 2195	2.6026 6011	3.1469 1674	3.8032 0888	4.5942 3521	77
78	1.7910 7708	2.1730 3717	2.6351 9336	3.1941 2050	3.8697 6503	4.6861 1991	78
79	1.8045 1015	2.1947 6754	2.6681 3327	3.2420 3230	3.9374 8592	4.7798 4231	79
80	1.8180 4398	2.2167 1522	2.7014 8494	3.2906 6279	4.0063 9192	4.8754 3916	80
81	1.8316 7931	2.2388 8237	2.7352 5350	3.3400 2273	4.0765 0378	4.9729 4794	81
82	1.8454 1691	2.2612 7119	2.7694 4417	3.3901 2307	4.1478 4260	5.0724 0690	82
83	1.8592 5753	2.2838 8390	2.8040 6222	3.4409 7492	4.2204 2984	5.1738 5504	83
84	1.8732 0196	2.3067 2274	2.8391 1300	3.4925 8954	4.2942 8737	5.2773 3224	84
85	1.8872 5098	2.3297 8997	2.8746 0191	3.5449 7838	4.3694 3740	5.3828 7878	85
86	1.9014 0536	2.3530 8787	2.9105 3444	3.5981 5306	4.4459 0255	5.4905 3636	86
87	1.9156 6590	2.3766 1875	2.9469 1612	3.6521 2535	4.5237 0584	5.6003 4708	87
88	1.9300 3339	2.4003 8494	2.9837 5257	3.7069 0723	4.6028 7070	5.7123 5402	88
89	1.9445 0865	2.4243 8879	3.0210 4948	3.7625 1084	4.6834 2093	5.8266 0110	89
90	1.9590 9246	2.4486 3267	3.0588 1260	3.8189 4851	4.7653 8080	5.9431 3313	90
91	1.9737 8565	2.4731 1900	3.0970 4775	3.8762 3273	4.8487 7496	6.0619 9579	91
92	1.9885 8905	2.4978 5019	3.1357 6085	3.9343 7622	4.9336 2853	6.1832 3570	92
93	2.0035 0346	2.5228 2869	3.1749 5786	3.9933 9187	5.0199 6703	6.3069 0042	93
94	2.0185 2974	2.5480 5698	3.2146 4483	4.0532 9275	5.1078 1645	6.4330 3843	94
95	2.0336 6871	2.5735 3755	3.2548 2789	4.1140 9214	5.1972 0324	6.5616 9920	95
96	2.0489 2123	2.5992 7293	3.2955 1324	4.1758 0352	5.2881 5429	6.6929 3318	96
97	2.0642 8814	2.6252 6565	3.3367 0716	4.2384 4057	5.3806 9699	6.8267 9184	97
98	2.0797 7030	2.6515 1831	3.3784 1600	4.3020 1718	5.4748 5919	6.9633 2768	98
99	2.0953 6858	2.6780 3349	3.4206 4620	4.3665 4744	5.5706 6923	7.1025 9423	99
100	2.1110 8384	2.7048 1383	3.4634 0427	4.4320 4565	5.6681 5594	7.2446 4612	100

TABLE I - AMOUNT OF 1

How $1 deposited at compound interest will grow

n	$2\frac{1}{2}\%$	3%	$3\frac{1}{2}\%$	4%	$4\frac{1}{2}\%$	5%	n
1	1.0250 0000	1.0300 0000	1.0350 0000	1.0400 0000	1.0450 0000	1.0500 0000	1
2	1.0506 2500	1.0609 0000	1.0712 2500	1.0816 0000	1.0920 2500	1.1025 0000	2
3	1.0768 9063	1.0927 2700	1.1087 1788	1.1248 6400	1.1411 6613	1.1576 2500	3
4	1.1038 1289	1.1255 0881	1.1475 2300	1.1698 5856	1.1925 1860	1.2155 0625	4
5	1.1314 0821	1.1592 7407	1.1876 8631	1.2166 5290	1.2461 8194	1.2762 8156	5
6	1.1596 9342	1.1940 5230	1.2292 5533	1.2653 1902	1.3022 6012	1.3400 9564	6
7	1.1886 8575	1.2298 7387	1.2722 7926	1.3159 3178	1.3608 6183	1.4071 0042	7
8	1.2184 0290	1.2667 7008	1.3168 0904	1.3685 6905	1.4221 0061	1.4774 5544	8
9	1.2488 6297	1.3047 7318	1.3628 9735	1.4233 1181	1.4860 9514	1.5513 2822	9
10	1.2800 8454	1.3439 1638	1.4105 9876	1.4802 4428	1.5529 6942	1.6288 9463	10
11	1.3120 8666	1.3842 3387	1.4599 6972	1.5394 5406	1.6228 5305	1.7103 3936	11
12	1.3448 8882	1.4257 6089	1.5110 6866	1.6010 3222	1.6958 8143	1.7958 5633	12
13	1.3785 1104	1.4685 3371	1.5639 5606	1.6650 7351	1.7721 9610	1.8856 4914	13
14	1.4129 7382	1.5125 8972	1.6186 9452	1.7316 7645	1.8519 4492	1.9799 3160	14
15	1.4482 9817	1.5579 6742	1.6753 4883	1.8009 4351	1.9352 8244	2.0789 2818	15
16	1.4845 0562	1.6047 0644	1.7339 8604	1.8729 8125	2.0223 7015	2.1828 7459	16
17	1.5216 1826	1.6528 4763	1.7946 7555	1.9479 0050	2.1133 7681	2.2920 1832	17
18	1.5596 5872	1.7024 3306	1.8574 8920	2.0258 1652	2.2084 7877	2.4066 1923	18
19	1.5986 5019	1.7535 0605	1.9225 0132	2.1068 4918	2.3078 6031	2.5269 5020	19
20	1.6386 1644	1.8061 1123	1.9897 8886	2.1911 2314	2.4117 1402	2.6532 9771	20
21	1.6795 8185	1.8602 9457	2.0594 3147	2.2787 6807	2.5202 4116	2.7859 6259	21
22	1.7215 7140	1.9161 0341	2.1315 1158	2.3699 1879	2.6336 5201	2.9252 6072	22
23	1.7646 1068	1.9735 8651	2.2061 1448	2.4647 1554	2.7521 6635	3.0715 2376	23
24	1.8087 2595	2.0327 9411	2.2833 2849	2.5633 0416	2.8760 1383	3.2250 9994	24
25	1.8539 4410	2.0937 7793	2.3632 4498	2.6658 3633	3.0054 3446	3.3863 5494	25
26	1.9002 9270	2.1565 9127	2.4459 5856	2.7724 6978	3.1406 7901	3.5556 7269	26
27	1.9478 0002	2.2212 8901	2.5315 6711	2.8833 6858	3.2820 0956	3.7334 5632	27
28	1.9964 9502	2.2879 2768	2.6201 7196	2.9987 0332	3.4296 9999	3.9201 2914	28
29	2.0464 0739	2.3565 6551	2.7118 7798	3.1186 5145	3.5840 3649	4.1161 3560	29
30	2.0975 6758	2.4272 6247	2.8067 9370	3.2433 9751	3.7453 1813	4.3219 4238	30
31	2.1500 0677	2.5000 8035	2.9050 3148	3.3731 3341	3.9138 5745	4.5380 3949	31
32	2.2037 5694	2.5750 8276	3.0067 0759	3.5080 5875	4.0899 8104	4.7649 4147	32
33	2.2588 5086	2.6523 3524	3.1119 4235	3.6483 8110	4.2740 3018	5.0031 8854	33
34	2.3153 2213	2.7319 0530	3.2208 6033	3.7943 1634	4.4663 6154	5.2533 4797	34
35	2.3732 0519	2.8138 6245	3.3335 9045	3.9460 8899	4.6673 4781	5.5160 1537	35
36	2.4325 3532	2.8982 7833	3.4502 6611	4.1039 3255	4.8773 7846	5.7918 1614	36
37	2.4933 4870	2.9852 2668	3.5710 2543	4.2680 8986	5.0968 6049	6.0814 0694	37
38	2.5556 8242	3.0747 8348	3.6960 1132	4.4388 1345	5.3262 1921	6.3854 7729	38
39	2.6195 7448	3.1670 2698	3.8253 7171	4.6163 6599	5.5658 9908	6.7047 5115	39
40	2.6850 6384	3.2620 3779	3.9592 5972	4.8010 2063	5.8163 6454	7.0399 8871	40
41	2.7521 9043	3.3598 9893	4.0978 3381	4.9930 6145	6.0781 0094	7.3919 8815	41
42	2.8209 9520	3.4606 9589	4.2412 5799	5.1927 8391	6.3516 1548	7.7615 8756	42
43	2.8915 2008	3.5645 1677	4.3897 0202	5.4004 9527	6.6374 3818	8.1496 6693	43
44	2.9638 0808	3.6714 5227	4.5433 4160	5.6165 1508	6.9361 2290	8.5571 5028	44
45	3.0379 0328	3.7815 9584	4.7023 5855	5.8411 7568	7.2482 4843	8.9850 0779	45
46	3.1138 5086	3.8950 4372	4.8669 4110	6.0748 2271	7.5744 1961	9.4342 5818	46
47	3.1916 9713	4.0118 9503	5.0372 8404	6.3178 1562	7.9152 6849	9.9059 7109	47
48	3.2714 8956	4.1322 5188	5.2135 8898	6.5705 2824	8.2714 5557	10.4012 6965	48
49	3.3532 7680	4.2562 1944	5.3960 6459	6.8333 4937	8.6436 7107	10.9213 3313	49
50	3.4371 0872	4.3839 0602	5.5849 2686	7.1066 8335	9.0326 3627	11.4673 9979	50

TABLE I - AMOUNT OF 1
How $1 deposited at compound interest will grow

n	$2\frac{1}{2}\%$	3%	$3\frac{1}{2}\%$	4%	$4\frac{1}{2}\%$	5%	n
51	3.5230 3644	4.5154 2320	5.7803 9930	7.3909 5068	9.4391 0490	12.0407 6978	51
52	3.6111 1235	4.6508 8590	5.9827 1327	7.6865 8871	9.8638 6463	12.6428 0826	52
53	3.7013 9016	4.7904 1247	6.1921 0824	7.9940 5226	10.3077 3853	13.2749 4868	53
54	3.7939 2491	4.9341 2485	6.4088 3202	8.3138 1435	10.7715 8677	13.9386 9611	54
55	3.8887 7303	5.0821 4859	6.6331 4114	8.6463 6692	11.2563 0817	14.6356 3092	55
56	3.9859 9236	5.2346 1305	6.8653 0108	8.9922 2160	11.7628 4204	15.3674 1246	56
57	4.0856 4217	5.3916 5144	7.1055 8662	9.3519 1046	12.2921 6993	16.1357 8309	57
58	4.1877 8322	5.5534 0098	7.3542 8215	9.7259 8688	12.8453 1758	16.9425 7224	58
59	4.2924 7780	5.7200 0301	7.6116 8203	10.1150 2635	13.4233 5687	17.7897 0085	59
60	4.3997 8975	5.8916 0310	7.8780 9090	10.5196 2741	14.0274 0793	18.6791 8589	60
61	4.5097 8449	6.0683 5120	8.1538 2408	10.9404 1250	14.6586 4129	19.6131 4519	61
62	4.6225 2910	6.2504 0173	8.4392 0793	11.3780 2900	15.3182 8014	20.5938 0245	62
63	4.7380 9233	6.4379 1379	8.7345 8020	11.8331 5016	16.0076 0275	21.6234 9257	63
64	4.8565 4464	6.6310 5120	9.0402 9051	12.3064 7617	16.7279 4487	22.7046 6720	64
65	4.9779 5826	6.8299 8273	9.3567 0068	12.7987 3522	17.4807 0239	23.8399 0056	65
66	5.1024 0721	7.0348 8222	9.6841 8520	13.3106 8463	18.2673 3400	25.0318 9559	66
67	5.2299 6739	7.2459 2868	10.0231 3168	13.8431 1201	19.0893 6403	26.2834 9037	67
68	5.3607 1658	7.4633 0654	10.3739 4129	14.3968 3649	19.9483 8541	27.5976 6488	68
69	5.4947 3449	7.6872 0574	10.7370 2924	14.9727 0995	20.8460 6276	28.9775 4813	69
70	5.6321 0286	7.9178 2191	11.1128 2526	15.5716 1835	21.7841 3558	30.4264 2554	70
71	5.7729 0543	8.1553 5657	11.5017 7414	16.1944 8308	22.7644 2168	31.9477 4681	71
72	5.9172 2806	8.4000 1727	11.9043 3624	16.8422 6241	23.7888 2066	33.5451 3415	72
73	6.0651 5876	8.6520 1778	12.3209 8801	17.5159 5290	24.8593 1759	35.2223 9086	73
74	6.2167 8773	8.9115 7832	12.7522 2259	18.2165 9102	25.9779 8688	36.9835 1040	74
75	6.3722 0743	9.1789 2567	13.1985 5038	18.9452 5466	27.1469 9629	38.8326 8592	75
76	6.5315 1261	9.4542 9344	13.6604 9964	19.7030 6485	28.3686 1112	40.7743 2022	76
77	6.6948 0043	9.7379 2224	14.1386 1713	20.4911 8744	29.6451 9862	42.8130 3623	77
78	6.8621 7044	10.0300 5991	14.6334 6873	21.3108 3494	30.9792 3256	44.9536 8804	78
79	7.0337 2470	10.3309 6171	15.1456 4013	22.1632 6834	32.3732 9802	47.2013 7244	79
80	7.2095 6782	10.6408 9056	15.6757 3754	23.0497 9907	33.8300 9643	49.5614 4107	80
81	7.3898 0701	10.9601 1727	16.2243 8835	23.9717 9103	35.3524 5077	52.0395 1312	81
82	7.5745 5219	11.2889 2079	16.7922 4195	24.9306 6267	36.9433 1106	54.6414 8878	82
83	7.7639 1599	11.6275 8842	17.3799 7041	25.9278 8918	38.6057 6006	57.3735 6322	83
84	7.9580 1389	11.9764 1607	17.9882 6938	26.9650 0475	40.3430 1926	60.2422 4138	84
85	8.1569 6424	12.3357 0855	18.6178 5881	28.0436 0494	42.1584 5513	63.2543 5344	85
86	8.3608 8834	12.7057 7981	19.2694 8387	29.1653 4914	44.0555 8561	66.4170 7112	86
87	8.5699 1055	13.0869 5320	19.9439 1580	30.3319 6310	46.0380 8696	69.7379 2467	87
88	8.7841 5832	13.4795 6180	20.6419 5285	31.5452 4163	48.1098 0087	73.2248 2091	88
89	9.0037 6228	13.8839 4865	21.3644 2120	32.8070 5129	50.2747 4191	76.8860 6195	89
90	9.2288 5633	14.3004 6711	22.1121 7595	34.1193 3334	52.5371 0530	80.7303 6505	90
91	9.4595 7774	14.7294 8112	22.8861 0210	35.4841 0668	54.9012 7503	84.7668 8330	91
92	9.6960 6718	15.1713 6556	23.6871 1568	36.9034 7094	57.3718 3241	89.0052 2747	92
93	9.9384 6886	15.6265 0652	24.5161 6473	38.3796 0978	59.9535 6487	93.4554 8884	93
94	10.1869 3058	16.0953 0172	25.3742 3049	39.9147 9417	62.6514 7529	98.1282 6328	94
95	10.4416 0385	16.5781 6077	26.2623 2856	41.5113 8594	65.4707 9168	103.0346 7645	95
96	10.7026 4395	17.0755 0559	27.1815 1006	43.1718 4138	68.4169 7730	108.1864 1027	96
97	10.9702 1004	17.5877 7076	28.1328 6291	44.8987 1503	71.4957 4128	113.5957 3078	97
98	11.2444 6530	18.1154 0388	29.1175 1311	46.6946 6363	74.7130 4964	119.2755 1732	98
99	11.5255 7693	18.6588 6600	30.1366 2607	48.5624 5018	78.0751 3687	125.2392 9319	99
100	11.8137 1635	19.2186 3198	31.1914 0798	50.5049 4818	81.5885 1803	131.5012 5785	100

134

TABLE I - AMOUNT OF 1
How $1 deposited at compound interest will grow

n	5½%	6%	6½%	7%	7½%	8%	n
1	1.0550 0000	1.0600 0000	1.0650 0000	1.0700 0000	1.0750 0000	1.0800 0000	1
2	1.1130 2500	1.1236 0000	1.1342 2500	1.1449 0000	1.1556 2500	1.1664 0000	2
3	1.1742 4138	1.1910 1600	1.2079 4963	1.2250 4300	1.2422 9688	1.2597 1200	3
4	1.2388 2465	1.2624 7696	1.2864 6635	1.3107 9601	1.3354 6914	1.3604 8896	4
5	1.3069 6001	1.3382 2558	1.3700 8666	1.4025 5173	1.4356 2933	1.4693 2808	5
6	1.3788 4281	1.4185 1911	1.4591 4230	1.5007 3035	1.5433 0153	1.5868 7432	6
7	1.4546 7916	1.5036 3026	1.5539 8655	1.6057 8148	1.6590 4914	1.7138 2427	7
8	1.5346 8651	1.5938 4807	1.6549 9567	1.7181 8618	1.7834 7783	1.8509 3021	8
9	1.6190 9427	1.6894 7896	1.7625 7039	1.8384 5921	1.9172 3866	1.9990 0463	9
10	1.7081 4446	1.7908 4770	1.8771 3747	1.9671 5136	2.0610 3156	2.1589 2500	10
11	1.8020 9240	1.8982 9856	1.9991 5140	2.1048 5195	2.2156 0893	2.3316 3900	11
12	1.9012 0749	2.0121 9647	2.1290 9624	2.2521 9159	2.3817 7960	2.5181 7012	12
13	2.0057 7390	2.1329 2826	2.2674 8750	2.4098 4500	2.5604 1307	2.7196 2373	13
14	2.1160 9146	2.2609 0396	2.4148 7418	2.5785 3415	2.7524 4405	2.9371 9362	14
15	2.2324 7649	2.3965 5819	2.5718 4101	2.7590 3154	2.9588 7735	3.1721 6911	15
16	2.3552 6270	2.5403 5168	2.7390 1067	2.9521 6375	3.1807 9315	3.4259 4264	16
17	2.4848 0215	2.6927 7279	2.9170 4637	3.1588 1521	3.4193 5264	3.7000 1805	17
18	2.6214 6627	2.8543 3915	3.1066 5438	3.3799 3228	3.6758 0409	3.9960 1950	18
19	2.7656 4691	3.0255 9950	3.3085 8691	3.6165 2754	3.9514 8940	4.3157 0106	19
20	2.9177 5749	3.2071 3547	3.5236 4506	3.8696 8446	4.2478 5110	4.6609 5714	20
21	3.0782 3415	3.3995 6360	3.7526 8199	4.1405 6237	4.5664 3993	5.0338 3372	21
22	3.2475 3703	3.6035 3742	3.9966 0632	4.4304 0174	4.9089 2293	5.4365 4041	22
23	3.4261 5157	3.8197 4966	4.2563 8573	4.7405 2986	5.2770 9215	5.8714 6365	23
24	3.6145 8990	4.0489 3464	4.5330 5081	5.0723 6695	5.6728 7406	6.3411 8074	24
25	3.8133 9235	4.2918 7072	4.8276 9911	5.4274 3264	6.0983 3961	6.8484 7520	25
26	4.0231 2893	4.5493 8296	5.1414 9955	5.8073 5292	6.5557 1508	7.3963 5321	26
27	4.2444 0102	4.8223 4594	5.4756 9702	6.2138 6763	7.0473 9371	7.9880 6147	27
28	4.4778 4307	5.1116 8670	5.8316 1733	6.6488 3836	7.5759 4824	8.6271 0639	28
29	4.7241 2444	5.4183 8790	6.2106 7245	7.1142 5705	8.1441 4436	9.3172 7490	29
30	4.9839 5129	5.7434 9117	6.6143 6616	7.6122 5504	8.7549 5519	10.0626 5689	30
31	5.2580 6861	6.0881 0064	7.0442 9996	8.1451 1290	9.4115 7683	10.8676 6944	31
32	5.5472 6238	6.4533 8668	7.5021 7946	8.7152 7080	10.1174 4509	11.7370 8300	32
33	5.8523 6181	6.8405 8988	7.9898 2113	9.3253 3975	10.8762 5347	12.6760 4964	33
34	6.1742 4171	7.2510 2528	8.5091 5950	9.9781 1354	11.6919 7248	13.6901 3361	34
35	6.5138 2501	7.6860 8679	9.0622 5487	10.6765 8148	12.5688 7042	14.7853 4429	35
36	6.8720 8538	8.1472 5200	9.6513 0143	11.4239 4219	13.5115 3570	15.9681 7184	36
37	7.2500 5008	8.6360 8712	10.2786 3603	12.2236 1814	14.5249 0088	17.2456 2558	37
38	7.6488 0283	9.1542 5235	10.9467 4737	13.0792 7141	15.6142 6844	18.6252 7563	38
39	8.0694 8699	9.7035 0749	11.6582 8595	13.9948 2041	16.7853 3858	20.1152 9768	39
40	8.5133 0877	10.2857 1794	12.4160 7453	14.9744 5784	18.0442 3897	21.7245 2150	40
41	8.9815 4076	10.9028 6101	13.2231 1938	16.0226 6989	19.3975 5689	23.4624 8322	41
42	9.4755 2550	11.5570 3267	14.0826 2214	17.1442 5678	20.8523 7366	25.3394 8187	42
43	9.9966 7940	12.2504 5463	14.9979 9258	18.3443 5475	22.4163 0168	27.3666 4042	43
44	10.5464 9677	12.9854 8191	15.9728 6209	19.6284 5959	24.0975 2431	29.5559 7166	44
45	11.1265 5409	13.7646 1083	17.0110 9813	21.0024 5176	25.9048 3863	31.9204 4939	45
46	11.7385 1456	14.5904 8748	18.1168 1951	22.4726 2338	27.8477 0153	34.4740 8534	46
47	12.3841 3287	15.4659 1673	19.2944 1278	24.0457 0702	29.9362 7915	37.2320 1217	47
48	13.0652 6017	16.3938 7173	20.5485 4961	25.7289 0651	32.1815 0008	40.2105 7314	48
49	13.7838 4948	17.3775 0403	21.8842 0533	27.5299 2997	34.5951 1259	43.4274 1899	49
50	14.5419 6120	18.4201 5427	23.3066 7868	29.4570 2506	37.1897 4603	46.9016 1251	50

COMPOUND INTEREST

We will now discuss the second category of compound interest which is calculating the **present value of a future amount of money**.

The equation is $P = AC$

where P is the present value of money,
A is the future amount of money,
and C is a constant from the tables.

Let's start with the same problem we used as a previous example. Let's find the present value of a future amount of $1,489.85 at 5 years at 8% compounded monthly. Another way of thinking about this problem is, suppose you have a friend who will inherit $1,489.85 in exactly 5 years. How much could he sell the inheritance for today.

Our equation is $P = AC$. To find the constant C we will follow the same procedure as before. The tables we will use for this problem are **TABLE II** titled **Present Worth Of 1** . These tables are directly following this discussion beginning on page 138.

[1] Determine the interest rate PER PERIOD.
In this case the period is one month. Divide the interest rate by 12 and obtain 2/3%.
[2] Turn to the tables and locate the column titled 2/3%. (Page 139.)
[3] Now locate 60 (12 months x 5) under the n column and move across to the corresponding number under the 2/3% column. The number is 0.6712 1044 which is the **constant**.

[4] Substituting the constant in our equation gives:

$$P = AC$$
$$P = \$1{,}489.85 \times 0.6712\ 1044$$
$$P = \$1{,}000.00$$

Let's look at another problem. If we want to have $50,000 in 8 years, how much must we deposit today if money is worth 9%.

[1] Determine the interest rate PER PERIOD.
In this case the period is one month. Divide the interest rate by 12 and obtain 3/4%. (9% divided by 12.)
[2] Turn to the tables and locate the column titled 3/4%. (Page 142.)
[3] Now locate 96 (12 months x 8) under the n column and move across to the corresponding number under the 3/4% column. The number is 0.4880 6171 which is the constant.
[4] Substituting the constant in our equation gives:
$$P = AC$$
$$P = \$50{,}000.00 \times 0.4880\ 6171$$
$$P = \$24{,}403.09$$

By now this is becoming pretty easy. This concludes the discussion on compound interest. Next, we will learn about annuities. Turn to page 146 for this discussion.

TABLE II - PRESENT WORTH OF 1
What $1 due in the future is worth today

n	$\frac{1}{4}\%$	$\frac{1}{3}\%$	$\frac{5}{12}\%$	$\frac{1}{2}\%$	$\frac{7}{12}\%$	$\frac{2}{3}\%$	n
1	0.9975 0623	0.9966 7774	0.9958 5062	0.9950 2488	0.9942 0050	0.9933 7748	1
2	0.9950 1869	0.9933 6652	0.9917 1846	0.9900 7450	0.9884 3463	0.9867 9882	2
3	0.9925 3734	0.9900 6630	0.9876 0345	0.9851 4876	0.9827 0220	0.9802 6373	3
4	0.9900 6219	0.9867 7704	0.9835 0551	0.9802 4752	0.9770 0302	0.9737 7192	4
5	0.9875 9321	0.9834 9871	0.9794 2457	0.9753 7067	0.9713 3688	0.9673 2310	5
6	0.9851 3038	0.9802 3127	0.9753 6057	0.9705 1808	0.9657 0361	0.9609 1699	6
7	0.9826 7370	0.9769 7469	0.9713 1343	0.9656 8963	0.9601 0301	0.9545 5330	7
8	0.9802 2314	0.9737 2893	0.9672 8308	0.9608 8520	0.9545 3489	0.9482 3175	8
9	0.9777 7869	0.9704 9395	0.9632 6946	0.9561 0468	0.9489 9907	0.9419 5207	9
10	0.9753 4034	0.9672 6972	0.9592 7249	0.9513 4794	0.9434 9534	0.9357 1398	10
11	0.9729 0807	0.9640 5620	0.9552 9211	0.9466 1487	0.9380 2354	0.9295 1720	11
12	0.9704 8187	0.9608 5335	0.9513 2824	0.9419 0534	0.9325 8347	0.9233 6145	12
13	0.9680 6171	0.9576 6115	0.9473 8082	0.9372 1924	0.9271 7495	0.9172 4648	13
14	0.9656 4759	0.9544 7955	0.9434 4978	0.9325 5646	0.9217 9779	0.9111 7200	14
15	0.9632 3949	0.9513 0852	0.9395 3505	0.9279 1688	0.9164 5182	0.9051 3775	15
16	0.9608 3740	0.9481 4803	0.9356 3657	0.9233 0037	0.9111 3686	0.8991 4346	16
17	0.9584 4130	0.9449 9803	0.9317 5426	0.9187 0684	0.9058 5272	0.8931 8886	17
18	0.9560 5117	0.9418 5851	0.9278 8806	0.9141 3616	0.9005 9922	0.8872 7371	18
19	0.9536 6700	0.9387 2941	0.9240 3790	0.9095 8822	0.8953 7619	0.8813 9772	19
20	0.9512 8878	0.9356 1071	0.9202 0372	0.9050 6290	0.8901 8346	0.8755 6065	20
21	0.9489 1649	0.9325 0236	0.9163 8544	0.9005 6010	0.8850 2084	0.8697 6224	21
22	0.9465 5011	0.9294 0435	0.9125 8301	0.8960 7971	0.8798 8815	0.8640 0222	22
23	0.9441 8964	0.9263 1663	0.9087 9636	0.8916 2160	0.8747 8524	0.8582 8035	23
24	0.9418 3505	0.9232 3916	0.9050 2542	0.8871 8567	0.8697 1192	0.8525 9638	24
25	0.9394 8634	0.9201 7192	0.9012 7013	0.8827 7181	0.8646 6802	0.8469 5004	25
26	0.9371 4348	0.9171 1487	0.8975 3042	0.8783 7991	0.8596 5338	0.8413 4110	26
27	0.9348 0646	0.9140 6798	0.8938 0623	0.8740 0986	0.8546 6782	0.8357 6931	27
28	0.9324 7527	0.9110 3121	0.8900 9749	0.8696 6155	0.8497 1117	0.8302 3441	28
29	0.9301 4990	0.9080 0453	0.8864 0414	0.8653 3488	0.8447 8327	0.8247 3617	29
30	0.9278 3032	0.9049 8790	0.8827 2611	0.8610 2973	0.8398 8394	0.8192 7434	30
31	0.9255 1653	0.9019 8130	0.8790 6335	0.8567 4600	0.8350 1303	0.8138 4868	31
32	0.9232 0851	0.8989 8468	0.8754 1578	0.8524 8358	0.8301 7037	0.8084 5896	32
33	0.9209 0624	0.8959 9802	0.8717 8335	0.8482 4237	0.8253 5580	0.8031 0492	33
34	0.9186 0972	0.8930 2128	0.8681 6599	0.8440 2226	0.8205 6914	0.7977 8635	34
35	0.9163 1892	0.8900 5444	0.8645 6365	0.8398 2314	0.8158 1025	0.7925 0299	35
36	0.9140 3384	0.8870 9745	0.8609 7624	0.8356 4492	0.8110 7896	0.7872 5463	36
37	0.9117 5445	0.8841 5028	0.8574 0373	0.8314 8748	0.8063 7510	0.7820 4102	37
38	0.9094 8075	0.8812 1290	0.8538 4604	0.8273 5073	0.8016 9853	0.7768 6194	38
39	0.9072 1272	0.8782 8528	0.8503 0311	0.8232 3455	0.7970 4907	0.7717 1716	39
40	0.9049 5034	0.8753 6739	0.8467 7488	0.8191 3886	0.7924 2659	0.7666 0645	40
41	0.9026 9361	0.8724 5920	0.8432 6129	0.8150 6354	0.7878 3091	0.7615 2959	41
42	0.9004 4250	0.8695 6066	0.8397 6228	0.8110 0850	0.7832 6188	0.7564 8635	42
43	0.8981 9701	0.8666 7175	0.8362 7779	0.8069 7363	0.7787 1935	0.7514 7650	43
44	0.8959 5712	0.8637 9245	0.8328 0776	0.8029 5884	0.7742 0316	0.7464 9984	44
45	0.8937 2281	0.8609 2270	0.8293 5212	0.7989 6402	0.7697 1317	0.7415 5613	45
46	0.8914 9407	0.8580 6249	0.8259 1083	0.7949 8907	0.7652 4922	0.7366 4516	46
47	0.8892 7090	0.8552 1179	0.8224 8381	0.7910 3390	0.7608 1115	0.7317 6672	47
48	0.8870 5326	0.8523 7055	0.8190 7102	0.7870 9841	0.7563 9880	0.7269 2058	48
49	0.8848 4116	0.8495 3876	0.8156 7238	0.7831 8250	0.7520 1209	0.7221 0654	49
50	0.8826 3457	0.8467 1637	0.8122 8785	0.7792 8607	0.7476 5079	0.7173 2437	50

138

TABLE II - PRESENT WORTH OF 1
What $1 due in the future is worth today

n	$\frac{1}{4}\%$	$\frac{1}{3}\%$	$\frac{5}{12}\%$	$\frac{1}{2}\%$	$\frac{7}{12}\%$	$\frac{2}{3}\%$	n
51	0.8804 3349	0.8439 0336	0.8089 1736	0.7754 0902	0.7433 1479	0.7125 7388	51
52	0.8782 3790	0.8410 9969	0.8055 6086	0.7715 5127	0.7390 0393	0.7078 5485	52
53	0.8760 4778	0.8383 0534	0.8022 1828	0.7677 1270	0.7347 1808	0.7031 6707	53
54	0.8738 6312	0.8355 2027	0.7988 8957	0.7638 9324	0.7304 5708	0.6985 1033	54
55	0.8716 8391	0.8327 4446	0.7955 7468	0.7600 9277	0.7262 2079	0.6938 8444	55
56	0.8695 1013	0.8299 7787	0.7922 7354	0.7563 1122	0.7220 0907	0.6892 8918	56
57	0.8673 4178	0.8272 2047	0.7889 8610	0.7525 4847	0.7178 2178	0.6847 2435	57
58	0.8651 7883	0.8244 7222	0.7857 1230	0.7488 0445	0.7136 5877	0.6801 8975	58
59	0.8630 2128	0.8217 3311	0.7824 5208	0.7450 7906	0.7095 1990	0.6756 8518	59
60	0.8608 6911	0.8190 0310	0.7792 0539	0.7413 7220	0.7054 0504	0.6712 1044	60
61	0.8587 2230	0.8162 8216	0.7759 7217	0.7376 8378	0.7013 1404	0.6667 6534	61
62	0.8565 8085	0.8135 7026	0.7727 5237	0.7340 1371	0.6972 4677	0.6623 4968	62
63	0.8544 4474	0.8108 6737	0.7695 4593	0.7303 6190	0.6932 0308	0.6579 6326	63
64	0.8523 1395	0.8081 7346	0.7663 5279	0.7267 2826	0.6891 8285	0.6536 0588	64
65	0.8501 8848	0.8054 8850	0.7631 7291	0.7231 1269	0.6851 8593	0.6492 7737	65
66	0.8480 6831	0.8028 1246	0.7600 0621	0.7195 1512	0.6812 1219	0.6449 7752	66
67	0.8459 5343	0.8001 4531	0.7568 5266	0.7159 3544	0.6772 6150	0.6407 0614	67
68	0.8438 4382	0.7974 8702	0.7537 1219	0.7123 7357	0.6733 3372	0.6364 6306	68
69	0.8417 3947	0.7948 3756	0.7505 8476	0.7088 2943	0.6694 2872	0.6322 4807	69
70	0.8396 4037	0.7921 9690	0.7474 7030	0.7053 0291	0.6655 4637	0.6280 6100	70
71	0.8375 4650	0.7895 6502	0.7443 6876	0.7017 9394	0.6616 8653	0.6239 0165	71
72	0.8354 5786	0.7869 4188	0.7412 8009	0.6983 0243	0.6578 4908	0.6197 6985	72
73	0.8333 7442	0.7843 2745	0.7382 0424	0.6948 2829	0.6540 3388	0.6156 6542	73
74	0.8312 9618	0.7817 2171	0.7351 4115	0.6913 7143	0.6502 4081	0.6115 8816	74
75	0.8292 2312	0.7791 2463	0.7320 9078	0.6879 3177	0.6464 6973	0.6075 3791	75
76	0.8271 5523	0.7765 3618	0.7290 5306	0.6845 0923	0.6427 2053	0.6035 1448	76
77	0.8250 9250	0.7739 5632	0.7260 2794	0.6811 0371	0.6389 9307	0.5995 1769	77
78	0.8230 3491	0.7713 8504	0.7230 1537	0.6777 1513	0.6352 8723	0.5955 4738	78
79	0.8209 8246	0.7688 2230	0.7200 1531	0.6743 4342	0.6316 0288	0.5916 0336	79
80	0.8189 3512	0.7662 6807	0.7170 2770	0.6709 8847	0.6279 3990	0.5876 8545	80
81	0.8168 9289	0.7637 2233	0.7140 5248	0.6676 5022	0.6242 9816	0.5837 9350	81
82	0.8148 5575	0.7611 8505	0.7110 8960	0.6643 2858	0.6206 7754	0.5799 2732	82
83	0.8128 2369	0.7586 5619	0.7081 3902	0.6610 2346	0.6170 7792	0.5760 8674	83
84	0.8107 9670	0.7561 3574	0.7052 0069	0.6577 3479	0.6134 9917	0.5722 7159	84
85	0.8087 7476	0.7536 2366	0.7022 7454	0.6544 6248	0.6099 4118	0.5684 8171	85
86	0.8067 5787	0.7511 1993	0.6993 6054	0.6512 0644	0.6064 0382	0.5647 1693	86
87	0.8047 4600	0.7486 2451	0.6964 5863	0.6479 6661	0.6028 8698	0.5609 7709	87
88	0.8027 3915	0.7461 3739	0.6935 6876	0.6447 4290	0.5993 9054	0.5572 6201	88
89	0.8007 3731	0.7436 5853	0.6906 9088	0.6415 3522	0.5959 1437	0.5535 7153	89
90	0.7987 4046	0.7411 8790	0.6878 2495	0.6383 4350	0.5924 5836	0.5499 0549	90
91	0.7967 4859	0.7387 2548	0.6849 7090	0.6351 6766	0.5890 2240	0.5462 6374	91
92	0.7947 6168	0.7362 7125	0.6821 2870	0.6320 0763	0.5856 0636	0.5426 4610	92
93	0.7927 7973	0.7338 2516	0.6792 9829	0.6288 6331	0.5822 1014	0.5390 5241	93
94	0.7908 0273	0.7313 8720	0.6764 7962	0.6257 3464	0.5788 3361	0.5354 8253	94
95	0.7888 3065	0.7289 5735	0.6736 7265	0.6226 2153	0.5754 7666	0.5319 3629	95
96	0.7868 6349	0.7265 3556	0.6708 7733	0.6195 2391	0.5721 3918	0.5284 1353	96
97	0.7849 0124	0.7241 2182	0.6680 9361	0.6164 4170	0.5688 2106	0.5249 1410	97
98	0.7829 4388	0.7217 1610	0.6653 2143	0.6133 7483	0.5655 2218	0.5214 3785	98
99	0.7809 9140	0.7193 1837	0.6625 6076	0.6103 2321	0.5622 4243	0.5179 8462	99
100	0.7790 4379	0.7169 2861	0.6598 1155	0.6072 8678	0.5589 8171	0.5145 5426	100

TABLE II - PRESENT WORTH OF 1
What $1 due in the future is worth today

n	$\frac{1}{4}\%$	$\frac{1}{3}\%$	$\frac{5}{12}\%$	$\frac{1}{2}\%$	$\frac{7}{12}\%$	$\frac{2}{3}\%$	n
101	0.7771 0104	0.7145 4679	0.6570 7374	0.6042 6545	0.5557 3989	0.5111 4661	101
102	0.7751 6313	0.7121 7288	0.6543 4730	0.6012 5915	0.5525 1688	0.5077 6154	102
103	0.7732 3006	0.7098 0686	0.6516 3216	0.5982 6781	0.5493 1255	0.5043 9888	103
104	0.7713 0180	0.7074 4869	0.6489 2829	0.5952 9136	0.5461 2681	0.5010 5849	104
105	0.7693 7836	0.7050 9837	0.6462 3565	0.5923 2971	0.5429 5955	0.4977 4022	105
106	0.7674 5971	0.7027 5585	0.6435 5417	0.5893 8279	0.5398 1065	0.4944 4393	106
107	0.7655 4584	0.7004 2111	0.6408 8382	0.5864 5054	0.5366 8002	0.4911 6946	107
108	0.7636 3675	0.6980 9413	0.6382 2455	0.5835 3288	0.5335 6754	0.4879 1669	108
109	0.7617 3242	0.6957 7488	0.6355 7632	0.5806 2973	0.5304 7312	0.4846 8545	109
110	0.7598 3284	0.6934 6334	0.6329 3907	0.5777 4102	0.5273 9664	0.4814 7561	110
111	0.7579 3799	0.6911 5947	0.6303 1277	0.5748 6669	0.5243 3800	0.4782 8703	111
112	0.7560 4787	0.6888 6326	0.6276 9736	0.5720 0666	0.5212 9710	0.4751 1957	112
113	0.7541 6247	0.6865 7468	0.6250 9281	0.5691 6085	0.5182 7383	0.4719 7308	113
114	0.7522 8176	0.6842 9370	0.6224 9906	0.5663 2921	0.5152 6810	0.4688 4743	114
115	0.7504 0575	0.6820 2030	0.6199 1608	0.5635 1165	0.5122 7980	0.4657 4248	115
116	0.7485 3441	0.6797 5445	0.6173 4381	0.5607 0811	0.5093 0884	0.4626 5809	116
117	0.7466 6774	0.6774 9613	0.6147 8222	0.5579 1852	0.5063 5510	0.4595 9413	117
118	0.7448 0573	0.6752 4531	0.6122 3126	0.5551 4280	0.5034 1849	0.4565 5046	118
119	0.7429 4836	0.6730 0198	0.6096 9088	0.5523 8090	0.5004 9891	0.4535 2695	119
120	0.7410 9562	0.6707 6608	0.6071 6104	0.5496 3273	0.4975 9627	0.4505 2346	120
121	0.7392 4750	0.6685 3763	0.6046 4170	0.5468 9824	0.4947 1046	0.4475 3986	121
122	0.7374 0399	0.6663 1657	0.6021 3281	0.5441 7736	0.4918 4138	0.4445 7602	122
123	0.7355 6508	0.6641 0289	0.5996 3434	0.5414 7001	0.4889 8895	0.4416 3181	123
124	0.7337 3075	0.6618 9657	0.5971 4623	0.5387 7612	0.4861 5305	0.4387 0710	124
125	0.7319 0100	0.6596 9758	0.5946 6844	0.5360 9565	0.4833 3361	0.4358 0175	125
126	0.7300 7581	0.6575 0590	0.5922 0094	0.5334 2850	0.4805 3051	0.4329 1565	126
127	0.7282 5517	0.6553 2149	0.5897 4367	0.5307 7463	0.4777 4367	0.4300 4866	127
128	0.7264 3907	0.6531 4434	0.5872 9660	0.5281 3396	0.4749 7300	0.4272 0065	128
129	0.7246 2750	0.6509 7443	0.5848 5969	0.5255 0643	0.4722 1839	0.4243 7151	129
130	0.7228 2045	0.6488 1172	0.5824 3288	0.5228 9197	0.4694 7976	0.4215 6110	130
131	0.7210 1791	0.6466 5620	0.5800 1615	0.5202 9052	0.4667 5701	0.4187 6930	131
132	0.7192 1986	0.6445 0784	0.5776 0944	0.5177 0201	0.4640 5005	0.4159 9600	132
133	0.7174 2629	0.6423 6662	0.5752 1273	0.5151 2637	0.4613 5879	0.4132 4106	133
134	0.7156 3720	0.6402 3251	0.5728 2595	0.5125 6356	0.4586 8314	0.4105 0436	134
135	0.7138 5257	0.6381 0549	0.5704 4908	0.5100 1349	0.4560 2301	0.4077 8579	135
136	0.7120 7239	0.6359 8554	0.5680 8207	0.5074 7611	0.4533 7830	0.4050 8522	136
137	0.7102 9664	0.6338 7263	0.5657 2488	0.5049 5135	0.4507 4893	0.4024 0254	137
138	0.7085 2533	0.6317 6674	0.5633 7747	0.5024 3916	0.4481 3481	0.3997 3762	138
139	0.7067 5843	0.6296 6785	0.5610 3981	0.4999 3946	0.4455 3585	0.3970 9035	139
140	0.7049 9595	0.6275 7593	0.5587 1185	0.4974 5220	0.4429 5197	0.3944 6061	140
141	0.7032 3785	0.6254 9096	0.5563 9354	0.4949 7731	0.4403 8306	0.3918 4829	141
142	0.7014 8414	0.6234 1292	0.5540 8485	0.4925 1474	0.4378 2906	0.3892 5327	142
143	0.6997 3480	0.6213 4178	0.5517 8574	0.4900 6442	0.4352 8987	0.3866 7543	143
144	0.6979 8983	0.6192 7752	0.5494 9618	0.4876 2628	0.4327 6541	0.3841 1467	144
145	0.6962 4921	0.6172 2012	0.5472 1611	0.4852 0028	0.4302 5558	0.3815 7086	145
146	0.6945 1292	0.6151 6955	0.5449 4550	0.4827 8635	0.4277 6031	0.3790 4390	146
147	0.6927 8097	0.6131 2580	0.5426 8432	0.4803 8443	0.4252 7952	0.3765 3368	147
148	0.6910 5334	0.6110 8884	0.5404 3252	0.4779 9446	0.4228 1311	0.3740 4008	148
149	0.6893 3001	0.6090 5864	0.5381 9006	0.4756 1637	0.4203 6100	0.3715 6299	149
150	0.6876 1098	0.6070 3519	0.5359 5690	0.4732 5012	0.4179 2312	0.3691 0231	150

TABLE II - PRESENT WORTH OF 1
What $1 due in the future is worth today

n	$\frac{3}{4}\%$	1%	$1\frac{1}{4}\%$	$1\frac{1}{2}\%$	$1\frac{3}{4}\%$	2%	n
1	0.9925 5583	0.9900 9901	0.9876 5432	0.9852 2167	0.9828 0098	0.9803 9216	1
2	0.9851 6708	0.9802 9605	0.9754 6106	0.9706 6175	0.9658 9777	0.9611 6878	2
3	0.9778 3333	0.9705 9015	0.9634 1833	0.9563 1699	0.9492 8528	0.9423 2233	3
4	0.9705 5417	0.9609 8034	0.9515 2428	0.9421 8423	0.9329 5851	0.9238 4543	4
5	0.9633 2920	0.9514 6569	0.9397 7706	0.9282 6033	0.9169 1254	0.9057 3081	5
6	0.9561 5802	0.9420 4524	0.9281 7488	0.9145 4219	0.9011 4254	0.8879 7138	6
7	0.9490 4022	0.9327 1805	0.9167 1593	0.9010 2679	0.8856 4378	0.8705 6018	7
8	0.9419 7540	0.9234 8322	0.9053 9845	0.8877 1112	0.8704 1157	0.8534 9037	8
9	0.9349 6318	0.9143 3982	0.8942 2069	0.8745 9921	0.8554 4135	0.8367 5527	9
10	0.9280 0315	0.9052 8695	0.8831 8093	0.8616 6723	0.8407 2860	0.8203 4830	10
11	0.9210 9494	0.8963 2372	0.8722 7746	0.8489 3323	0.8262 6889	0.8042 6304	11
12	0.9142 3815	0.8874 4923	0.8615 0860	0.8363 8742	0.8120 5788	0.7884 9318	12
13	0.9074 3241	0.8786 6260	0.8508 7269	0.8240 2702	0.7980 9128	0.7730 3253	13
14	0.9006 7733	0.8699 6297	0.8403 6809	0.8118 4928	0.7843 6490	0.7578 7502	14
15	0.8939 7254	0.8613 4947	0.8299 9318	0.7998 5150	0.7708 7459	0.7430 1473	15
16	0.8873 1766	0.8528 2126	0.8197 4635	0.7880 3104	0.7576 1631	0.7284 4581	16
17	0.8807 1231	0.8443 7749	0.8096 2602	0.7763 8526	0.7445 8605	0.7141 6256	17
18	0.8741 5614	0.8360 1731	0.7996 3064	0.7649 1159	0.7317 7990	0.7001 5937	18
19	0.8676 4878	0.8277 3992	0.7897 5866	0.7536 0747	0.7191 9401	0.6864 3076	19
20	0.8611 8985	0.8195 4447	0.7800 0855	0.7424 7042	0.7068 2458	0.6729 7133	20
21	0.8547 7901	0.8114 3017	0.7703 7881	0.7314 9795	0.6946 6789	0.6597 7582	21
22	0.8484 1589	0.8033 9621	0.7608 6796	0.7206 8763	0.6827 2028	0.6468 3904	22
23	0.8421 0014	0.7954 4179	0.7514 7453	0.7100 3708	0.6709 7817	0.6341 5592	23
24	0.8358 3140	0.7875 6613	0.7421 9707	0.6995 4392	0.6594 3800	0.6217 2149	24
25	0.8296 0933	0.7797 6844	0.7330 3414	0.6892 0583	0.6480 9632	0.6095 3087	25
26	0.8234 3358	0.7720 4796	0.7239 8434	0.6790 2052	0.6369 4970	0.5975 7928	26
27	0.8173 0380	0.7644 0392	0.7150 4626	0.6689 8574	0.6259 9479	0.5858 6204	27
28	0.8112 1966	0.7568 3557	0.7062 1853	0.6590 9925	0.6152 2829	0.5743 7455	28
29	0.8051 8080	0.7493 4215	0.6974 9978	0.6493 5887	0.6046 4697	0.5631 1231	29
30	0.7991 8690	0.7419 2292	0.6888 8867	0.6397 6243	0.5942 4764	0.5520 7089	30
31	0.7932 3762	0.7345 7715	0.6803 8387	0.6303 0781	0.5840 2716	0.5412 4597	31
32	0.7873 3262	0.7273 0411	0.6719 8407	0.6209 9292	0.5739 8247	0.5306 3330	32
33	0.7814 7158	0.7201 0307	0.6636 8797	0.6118 1568	0.5641 1053	0.5202 2873	33
34	0.7756 5418	0.7129 7334	0.6554 9429	0.6027 7407	0.5544 0839	0.5100 2817	34
35	0.7698 8008	0.7059 1420	0.6474 0177	0.5938 6608	0.5448 7311	0.5000 2761	35
36	0.7641 4896	0.6989 2495	0.6394 0916	0.5850 8974	0.5355 0183	0.4902 2315	36
37	0.7584 6051	0.6920 0490	0.6315 1522	0.5764 4309	0.5262 9172	0.4806 1093	37
38	0.7528 1440	0.6851 5337	0.6237 1873	0.5679 2423	0.5172 4002	0.4711 8719	38
39	0.7472 1032	0.6783 6967	0.6160 1850	0.5595 3126	0.5083 4400	0.4619 4822	39
40	0.7416 4796	0.6716 5314	0.6084 1334	0.5512 6232	0.4996 0098	0.4528 9042	40
41	0.7361 2701	0.6650 0311	0.6009 0206	0.5431 1559	0.4910 0834	0.4440 1021	41
42	0.7306 4716	0.6584 1892	0.5934 8352	0.5350 8925	0.4825 6348	0.4353 0413	42
43	0.7252 0809	0.6518 9992	0.5861 5656	0.5271 8153	0.4742 6386	0.4267 6875	43
44	0.7198 0952	0.6454 4546	0.5789 2006	0.5193 9067	0.4661 0699	0.4184 0074	44
45	0.7144 5114	0.6390 5492	0.5717 7290	0.5117 1494	0.4580 9040	0.4101 9680	45
46	0.7091 3264	0.6327 2764	0.5647 1397	0.5041 5265	0.4502 1170	0.4021 5373	46
47	0.7038 5374	0.6264 6301	0.5577 4219	0.4967 0212	0.4424 6850	0.3942 6836	47
48	0.6986 1414	0.6202 6041	0.5508 5649	0.4893 6170	0.4348 5848	0.3865 3761	48
49	0.6934 1353	0.6141 1921	0.5440 5579	0.4821 2975	0.4273 7934	0.3789 5844	49
50	0.6882 5165	0.6080 3882	0.5373 3905	0.4750 0468	0.4200 2883	0.3715 2788	50

141

TABLE II - PRESENT WORTH OF 1
What $1 due in the future is worth today

n	$\frac{3}{4}\%$	1%	$1\frac{1}{4}\%$	$1\frac{1}{2}\%$	$1\frac{3}{4}\%$	2%	n
51	0.6831 2819	0.6020 1864	0.5307 0524	0.4679 8491	0.4128 0475	0.3642 4302	51
52	0.6780 4286	0.5960 5806	0.5241 5332	0.4610 6887	0.4057 0492	0.3571 0100	52
53	0.6729 9540	0.5901 5649	0.5176 8229	0.4542 5505	0.3987 2719	0.3500 9902	53
54	0.6679 8551	0.5843 1336	0.5112 9115	0.4475 4192	0.3918 6947	0.3432 3433	54
55	0.6630 1291	0.5785 2808	0.5049 7892	0.4409 2800	0.3851 2970	0.3365 0425	55
56	0.6580 7733	0.5728 0008	0.4987 4461	0.4344 1182	0.3785 0585	0.3299 0613	56
57	0.6531 7849	0.5671 2879	0.4925 8727	0.4279 9194	0.3719 9592	0.3234 3738	57
58	0.6483 1612	0.5615 1365	0.4865 0594	0.4216 6694	0.3655 9796	0.3170 9547	58
59	0.6434 8995	0.5559 5411	0.4804 9970	0.4154 3541	0.3593 1003	0.3108 7791	59
60	0.6386 9970	0.5504 4962	0.4745 6760	0.4092 9597	0.3531 3025	0.3047 8227	60
61	0.6339 4511	0.5449 9962	0.4687 0874	0.4032 4726	0.3470 5676	0.2988 0614	61
62	0.6292 2592	0.5396 0358	0.4629 2222	0.3972 8794	0.3410 8772	0.2929 4720	62
63	0.6245 4185	0.5342 6097	0.4572 0713	0.3914 1669	0.3352 2135	0.2872 0314	63
64	0.6198 9266	0.5289 7126	0.4515 6259	0.3856 3221	0.3294 5587	0.2815 7170	64
65	0.6152 7807	0.5237 3392	0.4459 8775	0.3799 3321	0.3237 8956	0.2760 5069	65
66	0.6106 9784	0.5185 4844	0.4404 8173	0.3743 1843	0.3182 2069	0.2706 3793	66
67	0.6061 5170	0.5134 1429	0.4350 4368	0.3687 8663	0.3127 4761	0.2653 3130	67
68	0.6016 3940	0.5083 3099	0.4296 7277	0.3633 3658	0.3073 6866	0.2601 2873	68
69	0.5971 6070	0.5032 9801	0.4243 6817	0.3579 6708	0.3020 8222	0.2550 2817	69
70	0.5927 1533	0.4983 1486	0.4191 2905	0.3526 7692	0.2968 8670	0.2500 2761	70
71	0.5883 0306	0.4933 8105	0.4139 5462	0.3474 6495	0.2917 8054	0.2451 2511	71
72	0.5839 2363	0.4884 9609	0.4088 4407	0.3423 3000	0.2867 6221	0.2403 1974	72
73	0.5795 7681	0.4836 5949	0.4037 9661	0.3372 7093	0.2818 3018	0.2356 0661	73
74	0.5752 6234	0.4788 7078	0.3988 1147	0.3322 8663	0.2769 8298	0.2309 8687	74
75	0.5709 7999	0.4741 2949	0.3938 8787	0.3273 7599	0.2722 1914	0.2264 5771	75
76	0.5667 2952	0.4694 3514	0.3890 2506	0.3225 3793	0.2675 3724	0.2220 1737	76
77	0.5625 1069	0.4647 8726	0.3842 2228	0.3177 7136	0.2629 3586	0.2176 6408	77
78	0.5583 2326	0.4601 8541	0.3794 7879	0.3130 7523	0.2584 1362	0.2133 9616	78
79	0.5541 6701	0.4556 2912	0.3747 9387	0.3084 4850	0.2539 6916	0.2092 1192	79
80	0.5500 4170	0.4511 1794	0.3701 6679	0.3038 9015	0.2496 0114	0.2051 0973	80
81	0.5459 4710	0.4466 5142	0.3655 9683	0.2993 9916	0.2453 0825	0.2010 8797	81
82	0.5418 8297	0.4422 2913	0.3610 8329	0.2949 7454	0.2410 8919	0.1971 4507	82
83	0.5378 4911	0.4378 5063	0.3566 2547	0.2906 1531	0.2369 4269	0.1932 7948	83
84	0.5338 4527	0.4335 1547	0.3522 2268	0.2863 2050	0.2328 6751	0.1894 8968	84
85	0.5298 7123	0.4292 2324	0.3478 7426	0.2820 8917	0.2288 6242	0.1857 7420	85
86	0.5259 2678	0.4249 7350	0.3435 7951	0.2779 2036	0.2249 2621	0.1821 3157	86
87	0.5220 1169	0.4207 6585	0.3393 3779	0.2738 1316	0.2210 5770	0.1785 6036	87
88	0.5181 2575	0.4165 9985	0.3351 4843	0.2697 6666	0.2172 5572	0.1750 5918	88
89	0.5142 6873	0.4124 7510	0.3310 1080	0.2657 7997	0.2135 1914	0.1716 2665	89
90	0.5104 4043	0.4083 9119	0.3269 2425	0.2618 5218	0.2098 4682	0.1682 6142	90
91	0.5066 4063	0.4043 4771	0.3228 8814	0.2579 8245	0.2062 3766	0.1649 6217	91
92	0.5028 6911	0.4003 4427	0.3189 0187	0.2541 6990	0.2026 9057	0.1617 2762	92
93	0.4991 2567	0.3963 8046	0.3149 6481	0.2504 1369	0.1992 0450	0.1585 5649	93
94	0.4954 1009	0.3924 5590	0.3110 7636	0.2467 1300	0.1957 7837	0.1554 4754	94
95	0.4917 2217	0.3885 7020	0.3072 3591	0.2430 6699	0.1924 1118	0.1523 9955	95
96	0.4880 6171	0.3847 2297	0.3034 4287	0.2394 7487	0.1891 0190	0.1494 1132	96
97	0.4844 2850	0.3809 1383	0.2996 9666	0.2359 3583	0.1858 4953	0.1464 8169	97
98	0.4808 2233	0.3771 4241	0.2959 9670	0.2324 4909	0.1826 5310	0.1436 0950	98
99	0.4772 4301	0.3734 0832	0.2923 4242	0.2290 1389	0.1795 1165	0.1407 9363	99
100	0.4736 9033	0.3697 1121	0.2887 3326	0.2256 2944	0.1764 2422	0.1380 3297	100

TABLE II - PRESENT WORTH OF 1
What $1 due in the future is worth today

n	2½%	3%	3½%	4%	4½%	5%	n
1	0.9756 0976	0.9708 7379	0.9661 8357	0.9615 3846	0.9569 3780	0.9523 8095	1
2	0.9518 1440	0.9425 9591	0.9335 1070	0.9245 5621	0.9157 2995	0.9070 2948	2
3	0.9285 9941	0.9151 4166	0.9019 4271	0.8889 9636	0.8762 9660	0.8638 3760	3
4	0.9059 5064	0.8884 8705	0.8714 4223	0.8548 0419	0.8385 6134	0.8227 0247	4
5	0.8838 5429	0.8626 0878	0.8419 7317	0.8219 2711	0.8024 5105	0.7835 2617	5
6	0.8622 9687	0.8374 8426	0.8135 0064	0.7903 1453	0.7678 9574	0.7462 1540	6
7	0.8412 6524	0.8130 9151	0.7859 9096	0.7599 1781	0.7348 2846	0.7106 8133	7
8	0.8207 4657	0.7894 0923	0.7594 1156	0.7306 9021	0.7031 8513	0.6768 3936	8
9	0.8007 2836	0.7664 1673	0.7337 3097	0.7025 8674	0.6729 0443	0.6446 0892	9
10	0.7811 9840	0.7440 9391	0.7089 1881	0.6755 6417	0.6439 2768	0.6139 1325	10
11	0.7621 4478	0.7224 2128	0.6849 4571	0.6495 8093	0.6161 9874	0.5846 7929	11
12	0.7435 5589	0.7013 7988	0.6617 8330	0.6245 9705	0.5896 6386	0.5568 3742	12
13	0.7254 2038	0.6809 5134	0.6394 0415	0.6005 7409	0.5642 7164	0.5303 2135	13
14	0.7077 2720	0.6611 1781	0.6177 8179	0.5774 7508	0.5399 7286	0.5050 6795	14
15	0.6904 6556	0.6418 6195	0.5968 9062	0.5552 6450	0.5167 2044	0.4810 1710	15
16	0.6736 2493	0.6231 6694	0.5767 0591	0.5339 0818	0.4944 6932	0.4581 1152	16
17	0.6571 9506	0.6050 1645	0.5572 0378	0.5133 7325	0.4731 7639	0.4362 9669	17
18	0.6411 6591	0.5873 9461	0.5383 6114	0.4936 2812	0.4528 0037	0.4155 2065	18
19	0.6255 2772	0.5702 8603	0.5201 5569	0.4746 4242	0.4333 0179	0.3957 3396	19
20	0.6102 7094	0.5536 7575	0.5025 6588	0.4563 8695	0.4146 4286	0.3768 8948	20
21	0.5953 8629	0.5375 4928	0.4855 7090	0.4388 3360	0.3967 8743	0.3589 4236	21
22	0.5808 6467	0.5218 9250	0.4691 5063	0.4219 5539	0.3797 0089	0.3418 4987	22
23	0.5666 9724	0.5066 9175	0.4532 8563	0.4057 2633	0.3633 5013	0.3255 7131	23
24	0.5528 7535	0.4919 3374	0.4379 5713	0.3901 2147	0.3477 0347	0.3100 6791	24
25	0.5393 9059	0.4776 0557	0.4231 4699	0.3751 1680	0.3327 3060	0.2953 0277	25
26	0.5262 3472	0.4636 9473	0.4088 3767	0.3606 8923	0.3184 0248	0.2812 4073	26
27	0.5133 9973	0.4501 8906	0.3950 1224	0.3468 1657	0.3046 9137	0.2678 4832	27
28	0.5008 7778	0.4370 7675	0.3816 5434	0.3334 7747	0.2915 7069	0.2550 9364	28
29	0.4886 6125	0.4243 4636	0.3687 4815	0.3206 5141	0.2790 1502	0.2429 4632	29
30	0.4767 4269	0.4119 8676	0.3562 7841	0.3083 1867	0.2670 0002	0.2313 7745	30
31	0.4651 1481	0.3999 8715	0.3442 3035	0.2964 6026	0.2555 0241	0.2203 5947	31
32	0.4537 7055	0.3883 3703	0.3325 8971	0.2850 5794	0.2444 9991	0.2098 6617	32
33	0.4427 0298	0.3770 2625	0.3213 4271	0.2740 9417	0.2339 7121	0.1998 7254	33
34	0.4319 0534	0.3660 4490	0.3104 7605	0.2635 5209	0.2238 9589	0.1903 5480	34
35	0.4213 7107	0.3553 8340	0.2999 7686	0.2534 1547	0.2142 5444	0.1812 9029	35
36	0.4110 9372	0.3450 3243	0.2898 3272	0.2436 6872	0.2050 2817	0.1726 5741	36
37	0.4010 6705	0.3349 8294	0.2800 3161	0.2342 9685	0.1961 9921	0.1644 3563	37
38	0.3912 8492	0.3252 2615	0.2705 6194	0.2252 8543	0.1877 5044	0.1566 0536	38
39	0.3817 4139	0.3157 5355	0.2614 1250	0.2166 2061	0.1796 6549	0.1491 4797	39
40	0.3724 3062	0.3065 5684	0.2525 7247	0.2082 8904	0.1719 2870	0.1420 4568	40
41	0.3633 4695	0.2976 2800	0.2440 3137	0.2002 7793	0.1645 2507	0.1352 8160	41
42	0.3544 8483	0.2889 5922	0.2357 7910	0.1925 7493	0.1574 4026	0.1288 3962	42
43	0.3458 3886	0.2805 4294	0.2278 0590	0.1851 6820	0.1506 6054	0.1227 0440	43
44	0.3374 0376	0.2723 7178	0.2201 0231	0.1780 4635	0.1441 7276	0.1168 6133	44
45	0.3291 7440	0.2644 3862	0.2126 5924	0.1711 9841	0.1379 6437	0.1112 9651	45
46	0.3211 4576	0.2567 3653	0.2054 6787	0.1646 1386	0.1320 2332	0.1059 9668	46
47	0.3133 1294	0.2492 5876	0.1985 1968	0.1582 8256	0.1263 3810	0.1009 4921	47
48	0.3056 7116	0.2419 9880	0.1918 0645	0.1521 9496	0.1208 9771	0.0961 4211	48
49	0.2982 1576	0.2349 5029	0.1853 2024	0.1463 4112	0.1156 9158	0.0915 6391	49
50	0.2909 4221	0.2281 0708	0.1790 5337	0.1407 1262	0.1107 0965	0.0872 0373	50

143

TABLE II - PRESENT WORTH OF 1
What $1 due in the future is worth today

n	2½%	3%	3½%	4%	4½%	5%	n
51	0.2838 4606	0.2214 6318	0.1729 9843	0.1353 0059	0.1059 4225	0.0830 5117	51
52	0.2769 2298	0.2150 1280	0.1671 4824	0.1300 9672	0.1013 8014	0.0790 9635	52
53	0.2701 6876	0.2087 5029	0.1614 9589	0.1250 9300	0.0970 1449	0.0753 2986	53
54	0.2635 7928	0.2026 7019	0.1560 3467	0.1202 8173	0.0928 3683	0.0717 4272	54
55	0.2571 5052	0.1967 6717	0.1507 5814	0.1156 5551	0.0888 3907	0.0683 2640	55
56	0.2508 7855	0.1910 3609	0.1456 6004	0.1112 0722	0.0850 1347	0.0650 7276	56
57	0.2447 5956	0.1854 7193	0.1407 3433	0.1069 3002	0.0813 5260	0.0619 7406	57
58	0.2387 8982	0.1800 6984	0.1359 7520	0.1028 1733	0.0778 4938	0.0590 2291	58
59	0.2329 6568	0.1748 2508	0.1313 7701	0.0988 6282	0.0744 9701	0.0562 1230	59
60	0.2272 8359	0.1697 3309	0.1269 3431	0.0950 6040	0.0712 8901	0.0535 3552	60
61	0.2217 4009	0.1647 8941	0.1226 4184	0.0914 0423	0.0682 1915	0.0509 8621	61
62	0.2163 3179	0.1599 8972	0.1184 9453	0.0878 8868	0.0652 8148	0.0485 5830	62
63	0.2110 5541	0.1553 2982	0.1144 8747	0.0845 0835	0.0624 7032	0.0462 4600	63
64	0.2059 0771	0.1508 0565	0.1106 1591	0.0812 5803	0.0597 8021	0.0440 4381	64
65	0.2008 8557	0.1464 1325	0.1068 7528	0.0781 3272	0.0572 0594	0.0419 4648	65
66	0.1959 8593	0.1421 4879	0.1032 6114	0.0751 2762	0.0547 4253	0.0399 4903	66
67	0.1912 0578	0.1380 0853	0.0997 6922	0.0722 3809	0.0523 8519	0.0380 4670	67
68	0.1865 4223	0.1339 8887	0.0963 9538	0.0694 5970	0.0501 2937	0.0362 3495	68
69	0.1819 9241	0.1300 8628	0.0931 3563	0.0667 8818	0.0479 7069	0.0345 0948	69
70	0.1775 5358	0.1262 9736	0.0899 8612	0.0642 1940	0.0459 0497	0.0328 6617	70
71	0.1732 2300	0.1226 1880	0.0869 4311	0.0617 4942	0.0439 2820	0.0313 0111	71
72	0.1689 9805	0.1190 4737	0.0840 0300	0.0593 7445	0.0420 3655	0.0298 1058	72
73	0.1648 7615	0.1155 7998	0.0811 6232	0.0570 9081	0.0402 2637	0.0283 9103	73
74	0.1608 5478	0.1122 1357	0.0784 1770	0.0548 9501	0.0384 9413	0.0270 3908	74
75	0.1569 3149	0.1089 4521	0.0757 6590	0.0527 8367	0.0368 3649	0.0257 5150	75
76	0.1531 0389	0.1057 7205	0.0732 0376	0.0507 5353	0.0352 5023	0.0245 2524	76
77	0.1493 6965	0.1026 9131	0.0707 2827	0.0488 0147	0.0337 3228	0.0233 5737	77
78	0.1457 2649	0.0997 0026	0.0683 3650	0.0469 2449	0.0322 7969	0.0222 4512	78
79	0.1421 7218	0.0967 9641	0.0660 2560	0.0451 1970	0.0308 8965	0.0211 8582	79
80	0.1387 0457	0.0939 7710	0.0637 9285	0.0433 8433	0.0295 5948	0.0201 7698	80
81	0.1353 2153	0.0912 3990	0.0616 3561	0.0417 1570	0.0282 8658	0.0192 1617	81
82	0.1320 2101	0.0885 8243	0.0595 5131	0.0401 1125	0.0270 6850	0.0183 0111	82
83	0.1288 0098	0.0860 0236	0.0575 3750	0.0385 6851	0.0259 0287	0.0174 2963	83
84	0.1256 5949	0.0834 9743	0.0555 9178	0.0370 8510	0.0247 8744	0.0165 9965	84
85	0.1225 9463	0.0810 6547	0.0537 1187	0.0356 5875	0.0237 2003	0.0158 0919	85
86	0.1196 0452	0.0787 0434	0.0518 9553	0.0342 8726	0.0226 9860	0.0150 5637	86
87	0.1166 8733	0.0764 1198	0.0501 4060	0.0329 6852	0.0217 2115	0.0143 3940	87
88	0.1138 4130	0.0741 8639	0.0484 4503	0.0317 0050	0.0207 8579	0.0136 5657	88
89	0.1110 6468	0.0720 2562	0.0468 0679	0.0304 8125	0.0198 9070	0.0130 0626	89
90	0.1083 5579	0.0699 2779	0.0452 2395	0.0293 0890	0.0190 3417	0.0123 8691	90
91	0.1057 1296	0.0678 9105	0.0436 9464	0.0281 8163	0.0182 1451	0.0117 9706	91
92	0.1031 3460	0.0659 1364	0.0422 1704	0.0270 9772	0.0174 3016	0.0112 3530	92
93	0.1006 1912	0.0639 9383	0.0407 8941	0.0260 5550	0.0166 7958	0.0107 0028	93
94	0.0981 6500	0.0621 2993	0.0394 1006	0.0250 5337	0.0159 6132	0.0101 9074	94
95	0.0957 7073	0.0603 2032	0.0380 7735	0.0240 8978	0.0152 7399	0.0097 0547	95
96	0.0934 3486	0.0585 6342	0.0367 8971	0.0231 6325	0.0146 1626	0.0092 4331	96
97	0.0911 5596	0.0568 5769	0.0355 4562	0.0222 7235	0.0139 8685	0.0088 0315	97
98	0.0889 3264	0.0552 0164	0.0343 4359	0.0214 1572	0.0133 8454	0.0083 8395	98
99	0.0867 6355	0.0535 9383	0.0331 8221	0.0205 9204	0.0128 0817	0.0079 8471	99
100	0.0846 4737	0.0520 3284	0.0320 6011	0.0198 0004	0.0122 5663	0.0076 0449	100

TABLE II - PRESENT WORTH OF 1

What $1 due in the future is worth today

n	$5\frac{1}{2}\%$	6%	$6\frac{1}{2}\%$	7%	$7\frac{1}{2}\%$	8%	n
1	0.9478 6730	0.9433 9623	0.9389 6714	0.9345 7944	0.9302 3256	0.9259 2593	1
2	0.8984 5242	0.8899 9644	0.8816 5928	0.8734 3873	0.8653 3261	0.8573 3882	2
3	0.8516 1366	0.8396 1928	0.8278 4909	0.8162 9788	0.8049 6057	0.7938 3224	3
4	0.8072 1674	0.7920 9366	0.7773 2309	0.7628 9521	0.7488 0053	0.7350 2985	4
5	0.7651 3435	0.7472 5817	0.7298 8084	0.7129 8618	0.6965 5863	0.6805 8320	5
6	0.7252 4583	0.7049 6054	0.6853 3412	0.6663 4222	0.6479 6152	0.6301 6963	6
7	0.6874 3681	0.6650 5711	0.6435 0621	0.6227 4974	0.6027 5490	0.5834 9040	7
8	0.6515 9887	0.6274 1237	0.6042 3119	0.5820 0910	0.5607 0223	0.5402 6888	8
9	0.6176 2926	0.5918 9846	0.5673 5323	0.5439 3374	0.5215 8347	0.5002 4897	9
10	0.5854 3058	0.5583 9478	0.5327 2604	0.5083 4929	0.4851 9393	0.4631 9349	10
11	0.5549 1050	0.5267 8753	0.5002 1224	0.4750 9280	0.4513 4319	0.4288 8286	11
12	0.5259 8152	0.4969 6936	0.4696 8285	0.4440 1196	0.4198 5413	0.3971 1376	12
13	0.4985 6068	0.4688 3902	0.4410 1676	0.4149 6445	0.3905 6198	0.3676 9792	13
14	0.4725 6937	0.4423 0096	0.4141 0025	0.3878 1724	0.3633 1347	0.3404 6104	14
15	0.4479 3305	0.4172 6506	0.3888 2652	0.3624 4602	0.3379 6602	0.3152 4170	15
16	0.4245 8109	0.3936 4628	0.3650 9533	0.3387 3460	0.3143 8699	0.2918 9047	16
17	0.4024 4653	0.3713 6442	0.3428 1251	0.3165 7439	0.2924 5302	0.2702 6895	17
18	0.3814 6590	0.3503 4379	0.3218 8969	0.2958 6392	0.2720 4932	0.2502 4903	18
19	0.3615 7906	0.3305 1301	0.3022 4384	0.2765 0833	0.2530 6913	0.2317 1206	19
20	0.3427 2896	0.3118 0473	0.2837 9703	0.2584 1900	0.2354 1315	0.2145 4821	20
21	0.3248 6158	0.2941 5540	0.2664 7608	0.2415 1309	0.2189 8897	0.1986 5575	21
22	0.3079 2567	0.2775 0510	0.2502 1228	0.2257 1317	0.2037 1067	0.1839 4051	22
23	0.2918 7267	0.2617 9726	0.2349 4111	0.2109 4688	0.1894 9830	0.1703 1528	23
24	0.2766 5656	0.2469 7855	0.2206 0198	0.1971 4662	0.1762 7749	0.1576 9934	24
25	0.2622 3370	0.2329 9863	0.2071 3801	0.1842 4918	0.1639 7906	0.1460 1790	25
26	0.2485 6275	0.2198 1003	0.1944 9579	0.1721 9549	0.1525 3866	0.1352 0176	26
27	0.2356 0450	0.2073 6795	0.1826 2515	0.1609 3037	0.1418 9643	0.1251 8682	27
28	0.2233 2181	0.1956 3014	0.1714 7902	0.1504 0221	0.1319 9668	0.1159 1372	28
29	0.2116 7944	0.1845 5674	0.1610 1316	0.1405 6282	0.1227 8761	0.1073 2752	29
30	0.2006 4402	0.1741 1013	0.1511 8607	0.1313 6712	0.1142 2103	0.0993 7733	30
31	0.1901 8390	0.1642 5484	0.1419 5875	0.1227 7301	0.1062 5212	0.0920 1605	31
32	0.1802 6910	0.1549 5740	0.1332 9460	0.1147 4113	0.0988 3918	0.0852 0005	32
33	0.1708 7119	0.1461 8622	0.1251 5925	0.1072 3470	0.0919 4343	0.0788 8893	33
34	0.1619 6321	0.1379 1153	0.1175 2042	0.1002 1934	0.0855 2877	0.0730 4531	34
35	0.1535 1963	0.1301 0522	0.1103 4781	0.0936 6294	0.0795 6164	0.0676 3454	35
36	0.1455 1624	0.1227 4077	0.1036 1297	0.0875 3546	0.0740 1083	0.0626 2458	36
37	0.1379 3008	0.1157 9318	0.0972 8917	0.0818 0884	0.0688 4729	0.0579 8572	37
38	0.1307 3941	0.1092 3885	0.0913 5134	0.0764 5686	0.0640 4399	0.0536 9048	38
39	0.1239 2362	0.1030 5552	0.0857 7590	0.0714 5501	0.0595 7580	0.0497 1341	39
40	0.1174 6314	0.0972 2219	0.0805 4075	0.0667 8038	0.0554 1935	0.0460 3093	40
41	0.1113 3947	0.0917 1905	0.0756 2512	0.0624 1157	0.0515 5288	0.0426 2123	41
42	0.1055 3504	0.0865 2740	0.0710 0950	0.0583 2857	0.0479 5617	0.0394 6411	42
43	0.1000 3322	0.0816 2962	0.0666 7559	0.0545 1268	0.0446 1039	0.0365 4084	43
44	0.0948 1822	0.0770 0908	0.0626 0619	0.0509 4643	0.0414 9804	0.0338 3411	44
45	0.0898 7509	0.0726 5007	0.0587 8515	0.0476 1349	0.0386 0283	0.0313 2788	45
46	0.0851 8965	0.0685 3781	0.0551 9733	0.0444 9859	0.0359 0961	0.0290 0730	46
47	0.0807 4849	0.0646 5831	0.0518 2848	0.0415 8747	0.0334 0428	0.0268 5861	47
48	0.0765 3885	0.0609 9840	0.0486 6524	0.0388 6679	0.0310 7375	0.0248 6908	48
49	0.0725 4867	0.0575 4566	0.0456 9506	0.0363 2410	0.0289 0582	0.0230 2693	49
50	0.0687 6652	0.0542 8836	0.0429 0616	0.0339 4776	0.0268 8913	0.0213 2123	50

ANNUITIES

An annuity is a sequence of payments made at equal intervals of time at the end of the period. In essence, it is compound interest on an amount that increases as each payment is made. For example, if you paid yourself $300 per month for 7 years at 8% interest, how much would you have.

The equation is S = RC

Where S is the future amount,
       R is the periodic payment,
and   C is a **constant** from the tables.

In this example R = $300, so the equation is:

$$S = \$300 \times C$$

To determine C, we use **TABLE III** titled **AMOUNT OF 1 PER PERIOD**. The table follows this discussion beginning on page 151.

[1] Determine the interest rate PER PERIOD.
    In this case the PERIOD is one month. Divide the interest rate b;y 12 and obtain 2/3%.
[2] Turn to the tables and locate the column titled 2/3%. (Page 152.)
[3] The column titled n stands for number of PERIODS. Move down to the number 84 (7 years x 12 periods) and under 2/3% you will see the **constant** 112.1133 0771.
[4] Multiplying the **constant** by $300.00 gives the future value of $33,633.99 rounded off to two decimal places.

$$P = RC$$

$$P = \$300 \times 112.11330771$$
$$P = \$33,633.99$$

As you can see, it's no more difficult to calculate an annuity then to calculate compound interest using the appropriate tables.

Now, let's calculate Mr. White's Plan. He makes $25,000 per year and he will pay himself 15% of that amount for the first 20 years and 20% the last 10 years. Money is worth 8%. Since our tables do not have enough periods to calculate it monthly (which is the way he does it) we will approximate the result by compounding it annually. Then, we will calculate it monthly (using tables not included here) and show the difference.

$$P = RC$$

Where R = $3,750 ($25,000 times 15%)
and   C a constant from the tables.

Following the same procedure as above we find the 8% column and 20 under the n column (page 158) and we find the constant 45.7619 6430.

Substituting in the equation we have:

$$P = \$3,750 \times 45.76196430$$
$$P = \$171,607.36$$

For the first 20 years

At this point, Mr. White will pay himself $5,000 per year ($25,000 times 20%) for the next 10 years. The way to handle this problem is to calculate the last ten years as a separate annuity and add it to the first annuity. However, the first annuity will continue to earn interest for the last ten years also. So we must calculate the compound interest on the first annuity ($171,607.36) and then add it to the second annuity.

For the second annuity R = $5,000. The period is 10 years and the interest rate is 8% per year.

$$P = RC$$

Where R = $5,000 ($25,000 times 20%)
and   C = a constant from the tables.

Following the same procedure as above we find the 8% column and 10 under the n column (page 158) and we find the constant 14.4865 6247.

Substituting in the equation we have:

$$P = \$5,000 \text{ x } 14.48656247$$
$$P = \mathbf{\$ \: 72,432.81}$$

Now we will calculate the compound interest for ten years on the first annuity. The compound interest equation is:

$$S = AC$$

Where A is $171,607.36
and   C is a constant from TABLE 1 (Page 135 under 8% where n is 10) the constant is 2.1589 2500.

Substituting in the equation we have:

$$S = \$171,607.36 \text{ x } 2.15892500$$
$$S = \mathbf{\$370,487.42}$$

148

Add to that   <u>72,432.81</u> (The second annuity)
               $442,920.23 Total for 30 years

Now we will show the result when this problem is calculated by compounding **monthly**.

First 20 years
$$P = RC$$
$$P = \$312.50 \times 589.020\ 415$$
$$P = \$184,068.88$$

Second 10 years
$$P = RC$$
$$P = \$416.66 \times 182.946\ 035\ 1817$$
$$P = \$76,226.29$$

Compound Interest on first annuity for last 10 years.

$$S = AC$$
$$S = \$184,068.88 \times 2.219\ 640\ 2345$$
$$S = \mathbf{\$408,566.65}$$

Add to that   <u>76,226.29</u> (The second annuity)
               $484,792.94 Total for 30 years

The actual amount of money Mr. White will obtain with his 30 year plan is $484,792.94 because the interest will be compounded monthly.

Suppose Mr. White should decide to continue his plan for 5 more years and instead of retiring at age 53 retire at age 58. Following is the problem with interest compounded monthly.

First 20 years
$$P = RC$$
$$P = \$312.50 \times 589.020\ 415$$
$$P = \$184,068.88$$

Second **15 years**

$$P = RC$$
$$P = \$416.66 \times 346.038\ 221\ 6115$$
$$P = \mathbf{\$144{,}180.28}$$

Compound Interest $S = AC$ on first annuity for last 15 years.

S =	$184,068.88	x 3.306 921 4774
S =	**$608,701.33**	
Add to that	144,180.28	(The second annuity)
	$752,881.61	Total for 35 years

With that we have completed the discussion on the **future value of an annuity**. The last category we will discuss is **the periodic payment for the future amount of an annuity** which follows on page 159.

TABLE 111 - AMOUNT OF 1 PER PERIOD
How $1 deposited periodically will grow

n	$\frac{1}{4}\%$	$\frac{1}{3}\%$	$\frac{5}{12}\%$	$\frac{1}{2}\%$	$\frac{7}{12}\%$	$\frac{2}{3}\%$	n
1	1.0000 0000	1.0000 0000	1.0000 0000	1.0000 0000	1.0000 0000	1.0000 0000	1
2	2.0025 0000	2.0033 3333	2.0041 6667	2.0050 0000	2.0058 3333	2.0066 6667	2
3	3.0075 0625	3.0100 1111	3.0125 1736	3.0150 2500	3.0175 3403	3.0200 4444	3
4	4.0150 2502	4.0200 4448	4.0250 6952	4.0301 0013	4.0351 3631	4.0401 7807	4
5	5.0250 6258	5.0334 4463	5.0418 4064	5.0502 5063	5.0586 7460	5.0671 1259	5
6	6.0376 2523	6.0502 2278	6.0628 4831	6.0755 0188	6.0881 8354	6.1008 9335	6
7	7.0527 1930	7.0703 9019	7.0881 1018	7.1058 7939	7.1236 9794	7.1415 6597	7
8	8.0703 5110	8.0939 5816	8.1176 4397	8.1414 0879	8.1652 5285	8.1891 7641	8
9	9.0905 2697	9.1209 3802	9.1514 6749	9.1821 1583	9.2128 8349	9.2437 7092	9
10	10.1132 5329	10.1513 4114	10.1895 9860	10.2280 2641	10.2666 2531	10.3053 9606	10
11	11.1385 3642	11.1851 7895	11.2320 5526	11.2791 6654	11.3265 1396	11.3740 9870	11
12	12.1663 8277	12.2224 6288	12.2788 5549	12.3355 6237	12.3925 8529	12.4499 2602	12
13	13.1967 9872	13.2632 0442	13.3300 1739	13.3972 4018	13.4648 7537	13.5329 2553	13
14	14.2297 9072	14.3074 1510	14.3855 5913	14.4642 2639	14.5434 2048	14.6231 4503	14
15	15.2653 6520	15.3551 0648	15.4454 9896	15.5365 4752	15.6282 5710	15.7206 3267	15
16	16.3035 2861	16.4062 9017	16.5098 5520	16.6142 3026	16.7194 2193	16.8254 3688	16
17	17.3442 8743	17.4609 7781	17.5786 4627	17.6973 0141	17.8169 5189	17.9376 0646	17
18	18.3876 4815	18.5191 8107	18.6518 9063	18.7857 8791	18.9208 8411	19.0571 9051	18
19	19.4336 1727	19.5809 1167	19.7296 0684	19.8797 1685	20.0312 5593	20.1842 3844	19
20	20.4822 0131	20.6461 8137	20.8118 1353	20.9791 1544	21.1481 0493	21.3188 0003	20
21	21.5334 0682	21.7150 0198	21.8985 2942	22.0840 1101	22.2714 6887	22.4609 2536	21
22	22.5872 4033	22.7873 8532	22.9897 7330	23.1944 3107	23.4013 8577	23.6106 6487	22
23	23.6437 0843	23.8633 4327	24.0855 6402	24.3104 0322	24.5378 9386	24.7680 6930	23
24	24.7028 1770	24.9428 8775	25.1859 2053	25.4319 5524	25.6810 3157	25.9331 8976	24
25	25.7645 7475	26.0260 3071	26.2908 6187	26.5591 1502	26.8308 3759	27.1060 7769	25
26	26.8289 8619	27.1127 8414	27.4004 0713	27.6919 1059	27.9873 5081	28.2867 8488	26
27	27.8960 5865	28.2031 6009	28.5145 7549	28.8303 7015	29.1506 1035	29.4753 6344	27
28	28.9657 9880	29.2971 7062	29.6333 8622	29.9745 2200	30.3206 5558	30.6718 6587	28
29	30.0382 1330	30.3948 2786	30.7568 5866	31.1243 9461	31.4975 2607	31.8763 4497	29
30	31.1133 0883	31.4961 4395	31.8850 1224	32.2800 1658	32.6812 6164	33.0888 5394	30
31	32.1910 9210	32.6011 3110	33.0178 6646	33.4414 1666	33.8719 0233	34.3094 4630	31
32	33.2715 6983	33.7098 0154	34.1554 4090	34.6086 2375	35.0694 8843	35.5381 7594	32
33	34.3547 4876	34.8221 6754	35.2977 5524	35.7816 6686	36.2740 6045	36.7750 9711	33
34	35.4406 3563	35.9382 4143	36.4448 2922	36.9605 7520	37.4856 5913	38.0202 6443	34
35	36.5292 3722	37.0580 3557	37.5966 8268	38.1453 7807	38.7043 2548	39.2737 3286	35
36	37.6205 6031	38.1815 6236	38.7533 3552	39.3361 0496	39.9301 0071	40.5355 5774	36
37	38.7146 1171	39.3088 3423	39.9148 0775	40.5327 8549	41.1630 2630	41.8057 9479	37
38	39.8113 9824	40.4398 6368	41.0811 1945	41.7354 4942	42.4031 4395	43.0845 0009	38
39	40.9109 2673	41.5746 6322	42.2522 9078	42.9441 2666	43.6504 9562	44.3717 3009	39
40	42.0132 0405	42.7132 4543	43.4283 4199	44.1588 4730	44.9051 2352	45.6675 4163	40
41	43.1182 3706	43.8556 2292	44.6092 9342	45.3796 4153	46.1670 7007	46.9719 9191	41
42	44.2260 3265	45.0018 0833	45.7951 6547	46.6065 3974	47.4363 7798	48.2851 3852	42
43	45.3365 9774	46.1518 1436	46.9859 7866	47.8395 7244	48.7130 9018	49.6070 3944	43
44	46.4499 3923	47.3056 5374	48.1817 5357	49.0787 7030	49.9972 4988	50.9377 5304	44
45	47.5660 6408	48.4633 3925	49.3825 1088	50.3241 6415	51.2889 0050	52.2773 3806	45
46	48.6849 7924	49.6248 8371	50.5882 7134	51.5757 8497	52.5880 8575	53.6258 5365	46
47	49.8066 9169	50.7902 9999	51.7990 5581	52.8336 6390	53.8948 4959	54.9833 5934	47
48	50.9312 0842	51.9596 0099	53.0148 8521	54.0978 3222	55.2092 3621	56.3499 1507	48
49	52.0585 3644	53.1327 9966	54.2357 8056	55.3683 2138	56.5312 9009	57.7255 8117	49
50	53.1886 8278	54.3099 0899	55.4617 6298	56.6451 6299	57.8610 5595	59.1104 1837	50

TABLE 111 — AMOUNT OF 1 PER PERIOD
How $1 deposited periodically will grow

n	$\frac{1}{4}\%$	$\frac{1}{3}\%$	$\frac{5}{12}\%$	$\frac{1}{2}\%$	$\frac{7}{12}\%$	$\frac{2}{3}\%$	n
51	54.3216 5449	55.4909 4202	56.6928 5366	57.9283 8880	59.1985 7877	60.5044 8783	51
52	55.4574 5862	56.6759 1183	57.9290 7388	59.2180 3075	60.5439 0381	61.9078 5108	52
53	56.5961 0227	57.8648 3154	59.1704 4502	60.5141 2090	61.8970 7659	63.3205 7009	53
54	57.7375 9252	59.0577 1431	60.4169 8854	61.8166 9150	63.2581 4287	64.7427 0722	54
55	58.8819 365C	60.2545 7336	61.6687 2600	63.1257 7496	64.6271 4870	66.1743 2527	55
56	60.0291 4135	61.4554 2194	62.9256 7902	64.4414 0384	66.0041 4040	67.6154 8744	56
57	61.1792 1420	62.6602 7334	64.1878 6935	65.7636 1086	67.3891 6455	69.0662 5736	57
58	62.3321 6223	63.8691 4092	65.4553 1881	67.0924 2891	68.7822 6801	70.5266 9907	58
59	63.4879 9264	65.0820 3806	66.7280 4930	68.4278 9105	70.1834 9791	71.9968 7706	59
60	64.6467 1262	66.2989 7818	68.0060 8284	69.7700 3051	71.5929 0165	73.4768 5625	60
61	65.8083 2940	67.5199 7478	69.2894 4152	71.1188 8066	73.0105 2691	74.9667 0195	61
62	66.9728 5023	68.7450 4136	70.5781 4753	72.4744 7507	74.4364 2165	76.4664 7997	62
63	68.1402 8235	69.9741 9150	71.8722 2314	73.8368 4744	75.8706 3411	77.9762 5650	63
64	69.3106 3306	71.2074 3880	73.1716 9074	75.2060 3168	77.3132 1281	79.4960 9821	64
65	70.4839 0964	72.4447 9693	74.4765 7278	76.5820 6184	78.7642 0655	81.0260 7220	65
66	71.6601 1942	73.6862 7959	75.7868 9183	77.9649 7215	80.2236 6442	82.5662 4601	66
67	72.8392 6971	74.9319 0052	77.1026 7055	79.3547 9701	81.6916 3580	84.1166 8765	67
68	74.0213 6789	76.1816 7352	78.4239 3168	80.7515 7099	83.1681 7034	85.6774 6557	68
69	75.2064 2131	77.4356 1243	79.7506 9806	82.1553 2885	84.6533 1800	87.2486 4867	69
70	76.3944 3736	78.6937 3114	81.0829 9264	83.5661 0549	86.1471 2902	88.8303 0633	70
71	77.5854 2345	79.9560 4358	82.4208 3844	84.9839 3602	87.6496 5394	90.4225 0837	71
72	78.7793 8701	81.2225 6372	83.7642 5860	86.4088 5570	89.1609 4359	92.0253 2510	72
73	79.9763 3548	82.4933 0560	85.1132 7634	87.8408 9998	90.6810 4909	93.6388 2726	73
74	81.1762 7632	83.7682 8329	86.4679 1499	89.2801 0448	92.2100 2188	95.2630 8611	74
75	82.3792 1701	85.0475 1090	87.8281 9797	90.7265 0500	93.7479 1367	96.8981 7335	75
76	83.5851 6505	86.3310 0260	89.1941 4880	92.1801 3752	95.2947 7650	98.5441 6118	76
77	84.7941 2797	87.6187 7261	90.5657 9108	93.6410 3821	96.8506 6270	100.2011 2225	77
78	86.0061 1329	88.9108 3519	91.9431 4855	95.1092 4340	98.4156 2490	101.8691 2973	78
79	87.2211 2857	90.2072 0464	93.3262 450C	96.5847 8962	99.9897 1604	103.5482 5726	79
80	88.4391 8139	91.5078 9532	94.7151 0435	98.0677 1357	101.5729 8939	105.2385 7898	80
81	89.6602 7934	92.8129 2164	96.1097 5062	99.5580 5214	103.1654 9849	106.9401 6950	81
82	90.8844 3004	94.1222 9804	97.5102 0792	101.0558 4240	104.7672 9723	108.6531 0397	82
83	92.1116 4112	95.4360 3904	98.9165 0045	102.5611 2161	106.3784 3980	110.3774 5799	83
84	93.3419 2022	96.7541 5917	100.3286 5253	104.0739 2722	107.9989 8070	112.1133 0771	84
85	94.5752 7502	98.0766 7303	101.7466 8859	105.5942 9685	109.6289 7475	113.8607 2977	85
86	95.8117 1321	99.4035 9527	103.1706 3312	107.1222 6834	111.2684 7710	115.6198 0130	86
87	97.0512 4249	100.7349 4059	104.6005 1076	108.6578 7968	112.9175 4322	117.3905 9997	87
88	98.2938 7060	102.0707 2373	106.0363 4622	110.2011 6908	114.5762 2889	119.1732 0397	88
89	99.5396 0527	103.4109 5947	107.4781 6433	111.7521 7492	116.2445 9022	120.9676 9200	89
90	100.7884 5429	104.7556 6267	108.9259 9002	113.3109 3580	117.9226 8367	122.7741 4328	90
91	102.0404 2542	106.1048 4821	110.3798 4831	114.8774 9048	119.6105 6599	124.5926 3757	91
92	103.2955 2649	107.4585 3104	111.8397 6434	116.4518 7793	121.3082 9429	126.4232 5515	92
93	104.5537 6530	108.8167 2614	113.3057 6326	118.0341 3732	123.0159 2601	128.2660 7685	93
94	105.8151 4972	110.1794 4856	114.7778 7071	119.6243 0800	124.7335 1891	130.1211 8403	94
95	107.0796 8759	111.5467 1339	116.2561 1184	121.2224 2954	126.4611 3110	131.9886 5859	95
96	108.3473 8681	112.9185 3577	117.7405 1230	122.8285 4169	128.1988 2103	133.8685 8298	96
97	109.6182 5528	114.2949 3089	119.2310 9777	124.4426 8440	129.9466 4749	135.7610 4020	97
98	110.8923 0091	115.6759 1399	120.7278 9401	126.0648 9782	131.7046 6960	137.6661 1380	98
99	112.1695 3167	117.0615 0037	122.2309 2690	127.6952 2231	133.4729 4684	139.5838 8790	99
100	113.4499 5550	118.4517 0537	123.7402 2243	129.3336 9842	135.2515 3903	141.5144 4715	100

152

TABLE 111 - AMOUNT OF 1 PER PERIOD
How $1 deposited periodically will grow

n	$\frac{1}{4}\%$	$\frac{1}{3}\%$	$\frac{5}{12}\%$	$\frac{1}{2}\%$	$\frac{7}{12}\%$	$\frac{2}{3}\%$	n
101	114.7335 8038	119.8465 4439	125.2558 0669	130.9803 6692	137.0405 0634	143.4578 7680	101
102	116.0204 1434	121.2460 3287	126.7777 0589	132.6352 6875	138.8399 0929	145.4142 6264	102
103	117.3104 6537	122.6501 8632	128.3059 4633	134.2984 4509	140.6498 0877	147.3836 9106	103
104	118.6037 4153	124.0590 2027	129.8405 5444	135.9699 3732	142.4702 6598	149.3662 4900	104
105	119.9002 5089	125.4725 5034	131.3815 5675	137.6497 8701	144.3013 4253	151.3620 2399	105
106	121.2000 0152	126.8907 9217	132.9289 7990	139.3380 3594	146.1431 0037	153.3711 0415	106
107	122.5030 0152	128.3137 6148	134.4828 5065	141.0347 2612	147.9956 0178	155.3935 7818	107
108	123.8092 5902	129.7414 7402	136.0431 9586	142.7398 9975	149.8589 0946	157.4295 3537	108
109	125.1187 8217	131.1739 4560	137.6100 4251	144.4535 9925	151.7330.8643	159.4790 6560	109
110	126.4315 7913	132.6111 9208	139.1834 1769	146.1758 6725	153.6181 9610	161.5422 5937	110
111	127.7476 5807	134.0532 2939	140.7633 4859	147.9067 4658	155.5143 0225	163.6192 0777	111
112	129.0670 2722	135.5000 7349	142.3498 6255	149.6462 8032	157.4214 6901	165.7100 0249	112
113	130.3896 9479	136.9517 4040	143.9429 8697	151.3945 1172	159.3397 6091	167.8147 3584	113
114	131.7156 6902	138.4082 4620	145.5427 4942	153.1514 8428	161.2692 4285	169.9335 0074	114
115	133.0449 5820	139.8696 0702	147.1491 7754	154.9172 4170	163.2099 8010	172.0663 9075	115
116	134.3775 7059	141.3358 3905	148.7622 9911	156.6918 2791	165.1620 3832	174.2135 0002	116
117	135.7135 1452	142.8069 5851	150.3821 4203	158.4752 8704	167.1254 8354	176.3749 2335	117
118	137.0527 9830	144.2829 8170	152.0087 3429	160.2676 6348	169.1003 8220	178.5507 5618	118
119	138.3954 3030	145.7639 2498	153.6421 0401	162.0690 0180	171.0868 0109	180.7410 9455	119
120	139.7414 1888	147.2498 0473	155.2822 7945	163.8793 4681	173.0848 0743	182.9460 3518	120
121	141.0907 7242	148.7406 3741	156.9292 8894	165.6987 4354	175.0944 6881	185.1656 7542	121
122	142.4434 9935	150.2364 3953	158.5831 6098	167.5272 3726	177.1158 5321	187.4001 1325	122
123	143.7996 0810	151.7372 2766	160.2439 2415	169.3648 7344	179.1490 2902	189.6494 4734	123
124	145.1591 0712	153.2430 1842	161.9116 0717	171.2116 9781	181.1940 6502	191.9137 7699	124
125	146.5220 0489	154.7538 2848	163.5862 3887	173.0677 5630	183.2510 3040	194.1932 0217	125
126	147.8883 0990	156.2696 7458	165.2678 4819	174.9330 9508	185.3199 9475	196.4878 2352	126
127	149.2580 3068	157.7905 7349	166.9564 6423	176.8077 6056	187.4010 2805	198.7977 4234	127
128	150.6311 7575	159.3165 4207	168.6521 1616	178.6917 9936	189.4942 0071	201.1230 6062	128
129	152.0077 5369	160.8475 9721	170.3548 3331	180.5852 5836	191.5995 8355	203.4638 8103	129
130	153.3877 7308	162.3837 5587	172.0646 4512	182.4881 8465	193.7172 4779	205.8203 0690	130
131	154.7712 4251	163.9250 3506	173.7815 8114	184.4006 2557	195.8472 6507	208.1924 4228	131
132	156.1581 7062	165.4714 5184	175.5056 7106	186.3226 2870	197.9897 0745	210.5803 9190	132
133	157.5485 6604	167.0230 2335	177.2369 4469	188.2542 4184	200.1446 4741	212.9842 6117	133
134	158.9424 3746	168.5797 6676	178.9754 3196	190.1955 1305	202.3121 5785	215.4041 5625	134
135	160.3397 9355	170.1416 9931	180.7211 6293	192.1464 9062	204.4923 1210	217.8401 8396	135
136	161.7406 4304	171.7088 3831	182.4741 6777	194.1072 2307	206.6851 8393	220.2924 5185	136
137	163.1449 9464	173.2812 0111	184.2344 7680	196.0777 5919	208.8908 4750	222.7610 6820	137
138	164.5528 5713	174.8588 0511	186.0021 2046	198.0581 4798	211.1093 7744	225.2461 4198	138
139	165.9642 3927	176.4416 6779	187.7771 2929	200.0484 3872	213.3408 4881	227.7477 8293	139
140	167.3791 4987	178.0298 0669	189.5595 3400	202.0486 8092	215.5853 3710	230.2661 0148	140
141	168.7975 9775	179.6232 3937	191.3493 6539	204.0589 2432	217.8429 1823	232.8012 0883	141
142	170.2195 9174	181.2219 8351	193.1466 5441	206.0792 1894	220.1136 6858	235.3532 1688	142
143	171.6451 4072	182.8260 5678	194.9514 3214	208.1096 1504	222.3976 6498	237.9222 3833	143
144	173.0742 5357	184.4354 7697	196.7637 2977	210.1501 6311	224.6949 8470	240.5083 8659	144
145	174.5069 3921	186.0502 6190	198.5835 7865	212.2009 1393	227.0057 0544	243.1117 7583	145
146	175.9432 0655	187.6704 2944	200.4110 1023	214.2619 1850	229.3299 0539	245.7325 2100	146
147	177.3830 6457	189.2959 9753	202.2460 5610	216.3332 2809	231.6676 6317	248.3707 3781	147
148	178.8265 2223	190.9269 8419	204.0887 4800	218.4148 9423	234.0190 5787	251.0265 4273	148
149	180.2735 8854	192.5634 0747	205.9391 1778	220.5069 6870	236.3841 6904	253.7000 5301	149
150	181.7242 7251	194.2052 8550	207.7971 9744	222.6095 0354	238.7630 7670	256.3913 8670	150

153

TABLE 111 - AMOUNT OF 1 PER PERIOD
How $1 deposited periodically will grow

n	$\frac{3}{4}\%$	1%	$1\frac{1}{4}\%$	$1\frac{1}{2}\%$	$1\frac{3}{4}\%$	2%	n
1	1.0000 0000	1.0000 0000	1.0000 0000	1.0000 0000	1.0000 0000	1.0000 0000	1
2	2.0075 0000	2.0100 0000	2.0125 0000	2.0150 0000	2.0175 0000	2.0200 0000	2
3	3.0225 5625	3.0301 0000	3.0376 5625	3.0452 2500	3.0528 0625	3.0604 0000	3
4	4.0452 2542	4.0604 0100	4.0756 2695	4.0909 0338	4.1062 3036	4.1216 0800	4
5	5.0755 6461	5.1010 0501	5.1265 7229	5.1522 6693	5.1780 8939	5.2040 4016	5
6	6.1136 3135	6.1520 1506	6.1906 5444	6.2295 5093	6.2687 0596	6.3081 2096	6
7	7.1594 8358	7.2135 3521	7.2680 3762	7.3229 9419	7.3784 0831	7.4342 8338	7
8	8.2131 7971	8.2856 7056	8.3588 8809	8.4328 3911	8.5075 3045	8.5829 6905	8
9	9.2747 7856	9.3685 2727	9.4633 7420	9.5593 3169	9.6564 1224	9.7546 2843	9
10	10.3443 3940	10.4622 1254	10.5816 6637	10.7027 2167	10.8253 9945	10.9497 2100	10
11	11.4219 2194	11.5668 3467	11.7139 3720	11.8632 6249	12.0148 4394	12.1687 1542	11
12	12.5075 8636	12.6825 0301	12.8603 6142	13.0412 1143	13.2251 0371	13.4120 8973	12
13	13.6013 9325	13.8093 2804	14.0211 1594	14.2368 2960	14.4565 4303	14.6803 3152	13
14	14.7034 0370	14.9474 2132	15.1963 7988	15.4503 8205	15.7095 3253	15.9739 3815	14
15	15.8136 7923	16.0968 9554	16.3863 3463	16.6821 3778	16.9844 4935	17.2934 1692	15
16	16.9322 8183	17.2578 6449	17.5911 6382	17.9323 6984	18.2816 7721	18.6392 8525	16
17	18.0592 7394	18.4304 4314	18.8110 5336	19.2013 5539	19.6016 0656	20.0120 7096	17
18	19.1947 1849	19.6147 4757	20.0461 9153	20.4893 7572	20.9446 3468	21.4123 1238	18
19	20.3386 7888	20.8108 9504	21.2967 6893	21.7967 1636	22.3111 6578	22.8405 5863	19
20	21.4912 1897	22.0190 0399	22.5629 7854	23.1236 6710	23.7016 1119	24.2973 6980	20
21	22.6524 0312	23.2391 9403	23.8450 1577	24.4705 2211	25.1163 8938	25.7833 1719	21
22	23.8222 9614	24.4715 8598	25.1430 7847	25.8375 7994	26.5559 2620	27.2989 8354	22
23	25.0009 6336	25.7163 0183	26.4573 6695	27.2251 4364	28.0206 5490	28.8449 6321	23
24	26.1884 7059	26.9734 6485	27.7880 8403	28.6335 2080	29.5110 1637	30.4218 6247	24
25	27.3848 8412	28.2431 9950	29.1354 3508	30.0630 2361	31.0274 5915	32.0302 9972	25
26	28.5902 7075	29.5256 3150	30.4996 2802	31.5139 6896	32.5704 3969	33.6709 0572	26
27	29.8046 9778	30.8208 8781	31.8808 7337	32.9866 7850	34.1404 2238	35.3443 2383	27
28	31.0282 3301	32.1290 9669	33.2793 8429	34.4814 7867	35.7378 7977	37.0512 1031	28
29	32.2609 4476	33.4503 8766	34.6953 7659	35.9987 0085	37.3632 9267	38.7922 3451	29
30	33.5029 0184	34.7848 9153	36.1290 6880	37.5386 8137	39.0171 5029	40.5680 7921	30
31	34.7541 7361	36.1327 4045	37.5806 8216	39.1017 6159	40.6999 5042	42.3794 4079	31
32	36.0148 2991	37.4940 6785	39.0504 4069	40.6882 8801	42.4121 9955	44.2270 2961	32
33	37.2849 4113	38.8690 0853	40.5385 7120	42.2986 1233	44.1544 1305	46.1115 7020	33
34	38.5645 7819	40.2576 9862	42.0453 0334	43.9330 9152	45.9271 1527	48.0338 0160	34
35	39.8538 1253	41.6602 7560	43.5708 6963	45.5920 8789	47.7308 3979	49.9944 7763	35
36	41.1527 1612	43.0768 7836	45.1155 0550	47.2759 6921	49.5661 2949	51.9943 6719	36
37	42.4613 6149	44.5076 4714	46.6794 4932	48.9851 0874	51.4335 3675	54.0342 5453	37
38	43.7798 2170	45.9527 2361	48.2926 4243	50.7198 8538	53.3336 2365	56.1149 3962	38
39	45.1081 7037	47.4122 5085	49.8862 2921	52.4806 8366	55.2669 6206	58.2372 3841	39
40	46.4464 8164	48.8863 7336	51.4895 5708	54.2678 9391	57.2341 3390	60.4019 8318	40
41	47.7948 3026	50.3752 3709	53.1331 7654	56.0819 1232	59.2357 3124	62.6100 2284	41
42	49.1532 9148	51.8789 8946	54.7973 4125	57.9231 4100	61.2723 5654	64.8622 2330	42
43	50.5219 4117	53.3977 7936	56.4823 0801	59.7919 8812	63.3446 2278	67.1594 6777	43
44	51.9008 5573	54.9317 5715	58.1883 3687	61.6888 6794	65.4531 5661	69.5026 5712	44
45	53.2901 1215	56.4810 7472	59.9156 9108	63.6142 0096	67.5985 8386	71.8927 1027	45
46	54.6897 8799	58.0458 8547	61.6646 3721	65.5684 1398	69.7815 5908	74.3305 6447	46
47	56.0999 6140	59.6263 4432	63.4354 4518	67.5519 4018	72.0027 3637	76.8171 7576	47
48	57.5207 1111	61.2226 0777	65.2283 8824	69.5652 1929	74.2627 8425	79.3535 1927	48
49	58.9521 1644	62.8348 3385	67.0437 4310	71.6086 9758	76.5623 8298	81.9405 8966	49
50	60.3942 5732	64.4631 8218	68.8817 8989	73.6828 2804	78.9022 2468	84.5794 0145	50

154

TABLE 111 - AMOUNT OF 1 PER PERIOD
How $1 deposited periodically will grow

n	$\frac{3}{4}\%$	1%	$1\frac{1}{4}\%$	$1\frac{1}{2}\%$	$1\frac{3}{4}\%$	2%	n
51	61.8472 1424	66.1078 1401	70.7428 1226	75.7880 7046	81.2830 1361	87.2709 8948	51
52	63.3110 6835	67.7688 9215	72.6270 9741	77.9248 9152	83.7054 6635	90.0164 0927	52
53	64.7859 0136	69.4465 8107	74.5349 3613	80.0937 6489	86.1703 1201	92.8167 3746	53
54	66.2717 9562	71.1410 4688	76.4666 2283	82.2951 7136	88.6782 9247	95.6730 7221	54
55	67.7688 3409	72.8524 5735	78.4224 5562	84.5295 9893	91.2301 6259	98.5865 3365	55
56	69.2771 0035	74.5809 8192	80.4027 3631	86.7975 4292	93.8266 9043	101.5582 6432	56
57	70.7966 7860	76.3267 9174	82.4077 7052	89.0995 0606	96.4686 5752	104.5894 2961	57
58	72.3276 5369	78.0900 5966	84.4378 6765	91.4359 9865	99.1568 5902	107.6812 1820	58
59	73.8701 1109	79.8709 6025	86.4933 4099	93.8075 3863	101.8921 0405	110.8348 4257	59
60	75.4241 3693	81.6696 6986	88.5745 0776	96.2146 5171	104.6752 1588	114.0515 3942	60
61	76.9898 1795	83.4863 6655	90.6816 8910	98.6578 7149	107.5070 3215	117.3325 7021	61
62	78.5672 4159	85.3212 3022	92.8152 1022	101.1377 3956	110.3884 0522	120.6792 2161	62
63	80.1564 9590	87.1744 4252	94.9754 0034	103.6548 0565	113.3202 0231	124.0928 0604	63
64	81.7576 6962	89.0461 8695	97.1625 9285	106.2096 2774	116.3033 0585	127.5746 6216	64
65	83.3708 5214	90.9366 4882	99.3771 2526	108.8027 7215	119.3386 1370	131.1261 5541	65
66	84.9961 3353	92.8460 1531	101.6193 3933	111.4348 1374	122.4270 3944	134.7486 7852	66
67	86.6336 0453	94.7744 7546	103.8895 8107	114.1063 3594	125.5695 1263	138.4436 5209	67
68	88.2833 5657	96.7222 2021	106.1882 0083	116.8179 3098	128.7669 7910	142.2125 2513	68
69	89.9454 8174	98.6894 4242	108.5155 5334	119.5701 9995	132.0204 0124	146.0567 7563	69
70	91.6200 7285	100.6763 3684	110.8719 9776	122.3637 5295	135.3307 5826	149.9779 1114	70
71	93.3072 2340	102.6831 0021	113.2578 9773	125.1992 0924	138.6990 4653	153.9774 6937	71
72	95.0070 2758	104.7099 3121	115.6736 2145	128.0771 9738	142.1262 7984	158.0570 1875	72
73	96.7195 8028	106.7570 3052	118.1195 4172	130.9983 5534	145.6134 8974	162.2181 5913	73
74	98.4449 7714	108.8246 0083	120.5960 3599	133.9633 3067	149.1617 2581	166.4625 2231	74
75	100.1833 1446	110.9128 4684	123.1034 8644	136.9727 8063	152.7720 5601	170.7917 7276	75
76	101.9346 8932	113.0219 7530	125.6422 8002	140.0273 7234	156.4455 6699	175.2076 0821	76
77	103.6991 9949	115.1521 9506	128.2128 0852	143.1277 8292	160.1833 6441	179.7117 6038	77
78	105.4769 4349	117.3037 1701	130.8154 6863	146.2746 9967	163.9865 7329	184.3059 9558	78
79	107.2680 2056	119.4767 5418	133.4506 6199	149.4688 2016	167.8563 3832	188.9921 1549	79
80	109.0725 3072	121.6715 2172	136.1187 9526	152.7108 5247	171.7938 2424	193.7719 5780	80
81	110.8905 7470	123.8882 3694	138.8202 8020	156.0015 1525	175.8002 1617	198.6473 9696	81
82	112.7222 5401	126.1271 1931	141.5555 3370	159.3415 3798	179.8767 1995	203.6203 4490	82
83	114.5676 7091	128.3883 9050	144.3249 7787	162.7316 6105	184.0245 6255	208.6927 5180	83
84	116.4269 2845	130.6722 7440	147.1290 4010	166.1726 3597	188.2449 9239	213.8666 0683	84
85	118.3001 3041	132.9789 9715	149.9681 5310	169.6652 2551	192.5392 7976	219.1439 3897	85
86	120.1873 8139	135.3087 8712	152.8427 5501	173.2102 0389	196.9087 1716	224.5268 1775	86
87	122.0887 8675	137.6618 7499	155.7532 8945	176.8083 5695	201.3546 1971	230.0173 5411	87
88	124.0044 5265	140.0384 9374	158.7002 0557	180.4604 8230	205.8783 2555	235.6177 0119	88
89	125.9344 8604	142.4388 7868	161.6839 5814	184.1673 8954	210.4811 9625	241.3300 5521	89
90	127.8789 9469	144.8632 6746	164.7050 0762	187.9299 0038	215.1646 1718	247.1566 5632	90
91	129.8380 8715	147.3119 0014	167.7638 2021	191.7488 4889	219.9299 9798	253.0997 8944	91
92	131.8118 7280	149.7850 1914	170.8608 6796	195.6250 8162	224.7787 7295	259.1617 8523	92
93	133.8004 6185	152.2828 6933	173.9966 2881	199.5594 5784	229.7124 0148	265.3450 2094	93
94	135.8039 6531	154.8056 9803	177.1715 8667	203.5528 4971	234.7323 6850	271.6519 2135	94
95	137.8224 9505	157.3537 5501	180.3862 3151	207.6061 4246	239.8401 8495	278.0849 5978	95
96	139.8561 6377	159.9272 9256	183.6410 5940	211.7202 3459	245.0373 8819	284.6466 5898	96
97	141.9050 8499	162.5265 6548	186.9365 7264	215.8960 3811	250.3255 4248	291.3395 9216	97
98	143.9693 7313	165.1518 3114	190.2732 7980	220.1344 7868	255.7062 3947	298.1663 8400	98
99	146.0491 4343	167.8033 4945	193.6516 9580	224.4364 9586	261.1810 9866	305.1297 1168	99
100	148.1445 1201	170.4813 8294	197.0723 4200	228.8030 4330	266.7517 6789	312.2323 0591	100

155

TABLE 111 - AMOUNT OF 1 PER PERIOD

How $1 deposited periodically will grow

n	$2\frac{1}{2}\%$	3%	$3\frac{1}{2}\%$	4%	$4\frac{1}{2}\%$	5%	n
1	1.0000 0000	1.0000 0000	1.0000 0000	1.0000 0000	1.0000 0000	1.0000 0000	1
2	2.0250 0000	2.0300 0000	2.0350 0000	2.0400 0000	2.0450 0000	2.0500 0000	2
3	3.0756 2500	3.0909 0000	3.1062 2500	3.1216 0000	3.1370 2500	3.1525 0000	3
4	4.1525 1563	4.1836 2700	4.2149 4288	4.2464 6400	4.2781 9113	4.3101 2500	4
5	5.2563 2852	5.3091 3581	5.3624 6588	5.4163 2256	5.4707 0973	5.5256 3125	5
6	6.3877 3673	6.4684 0988	6.5501 5218	6.6329 7546	6.7168 9166	6.8019 1281	6
7	7.5474 3015	7.6624 6218	7.7794 0751	7.8982 9448	8.0191 5179	8.1420 0845	7
8	8.7361 1590	8.8923 3605	9.0516 8677	9.2142 2626	9.3800 1362	9.5491 0888	8
9	9.9545 1880	10.1591 0613	10.3684 9581	10.5827 9531	10.8021 1423	11.0265 6432	9
10	11.2033 8177	11.4638 7931	11.7313 9316	12.0061 0712	12.2882 0937	12.5778 9254	10
11	12.4834 6631	12.8077 9569	13.1419 9192	13.4863 5141	13.8411 7879	14.2067 8716	11
12	13.7955 5297	14.1920 2956	14.6019 6164	15.0258 0546	15.4640 3184	15.9171 2652	12
13	15.1404 4179	15.6177 9045	16.1130 3030	16.6268 3768	17.1599 1327	17.7129 8285	13
14	16.5189 5284	17.0863 2416	17.6769 8636	18.2919 1119	18.9321 0937	19.5986 3199	14
15	17.9319 2666	18.5989 1389	19.2956 8088	20.0235 8764	20.7840 5429	21.5785 6359	15
16	19.3802 2483	20.1568 8130	20.9710 2971	21.8245 3114	22.7193 3673	23.6574 9177	16
17	20.8647 3045	21.7615 8774	22.7050 1575	23.6975 1239	24.7417 0689	25.8403 6636	17
18	22.3863 4871	23.4144 3537	24.4996 9130	25.6454 1288	26.8550 8370	28.1323 8467	18
19	23.9460 0743	25.1168 6844	26.3571 8050	27.6712 2940	29.0635 6246	30.5390 0391	19
20	25.5446 5761	26.8703 7449	28.2796 8181	29.7780 7858	31.3714 2277	33.0659 5410	20
21	27.1832 7405	28.6764 8572	30.2694 7068	31.9692 0172	33.7831 3680	35.7192 5181	21
22	28.8628 5590	30.5367 8030	32.3289 0215	34.2479 6979	36.3033 7795	38.5052 1440	22
23	30.5844 2730	32.4528 8370	34.4604 1373	36.6178 8858	38.9370 2996	41.4304 7512	23
24	32.3490 3798	34.4264 7022	36.6665 2821	39.0826 0412	41.6891 9631	44.5019 9887	24
25	34.1577 6393	36.4592 6432	38.9498 5669	41.6459 0829	44.5652 1015	47.7270 9882	25
26	36.0117 0803	38.5530 4225	41.3131 0168	44.3117 4462	47.5706 4460	51.1134 5376	26
27	37.9120 0073	40.7096 3352	43.7590 6024	47.0842 1440	50.7113 2361	54.6691 2645	27
28	39.8598 0075	42.9309 2252	46.2906 2734	49.9675 8298	53.9933 3317	58.4025 8277	28
29	41.8562 9577	45.2188 5020	48.9107 9930	52.9662 8630	57.4230 3316	62.3227 1191	29
30	43.9027 0316	47.5754 1571	51.6226 7728	56.0849 3775	61.0070 6966	66.4388 4750	30
31	46.0002 7074	50.0026 7818	54.4294 7098	59.3283 3526	64.7523 8779	70.7607 8988	31
32	48.1502 7751	52.5027 5852	57.3345 0247	62.7014 6867	68.6662 4524	75.2988 2937	32
33	50.3540 3445	55.0778 4128	60.3412 1005	66.2095 2742	72.7562 2628	80.0637 7084	33
34	52.6128 8531	57.7301 7652	63.4531 5240	69.8579 0851	77.0302 5646	85.0669 5938	34
35	54.9282 0744	60.4620 8181	66.6740 1274	73.6522 2486	81.4966 1800	90.3203 0735	35
36	57.3014 1263	63.2759 4427	70.0076 0318	77.5983 1385	86.1639 6581	95.8363 2272	36
37	59.7339 4794	66.1742 2259	73.4578 6930	81.7022 4640	91.0413 4427	101.6281 3886	37
38	62.2272 9664	69.1594 4927	77.0288 9472	85.9703 3626	96.1382 0476	107.7095 4580	38
39	64.7829 7906	72.2342 3275	80.7249 0604	90.4091 4971	101.4644 2398	114.0950 2309	39
40	67.4025 5354	75.4012 5973	84.5502 7775	95.0255 1570	107.0303 2306	120.7997 7424	40
41	70.0876 1737	78.6632 9753	88.5095 3747	99.8265 3633	112.8466 8760	127.8397 6295	41
42	72.8398 0781	82.0231 9645	92.6073 7128	104.8195 9778	118.9247 8854	135.2317 5110	42
43	75.6608 0300	85.4838 9234	96.8486 2928	110.0123 8169	125.2764 0402	142.9933 3866	43
44	78.5523 2308	89.0484 0911	101.2383 3130	115.4128 7696	131.9138 4220	151.1430 0559	44
45	81.5161 3116	92.7198 6139	105.7816 7290	121.0293 9204	138.8499 6510	159.7001 5587	45
46	84.5540 3443	96.5014 5723	110.4840 3145	126.8705 6772	146.0982 1353	168.6851 6366	46
47	87.6678 8530	100.3965 0095	115.3509 7255	132.9453 9043	153.6726 3314	178.1194 2185	47
48	90.8595 8243	104.4083 9598	120.3882 5659	139.2632 0604	161.5879 0163	188.0253 9294	48
49	94.1310 7199	108.5406 4785	125.6018 4557	145.8337 3429	169.8593 5720	198.4266 6259	49
50	97.4843 4879	112.7968 6729	130.9979 1016	152.6670 8366	178.5030 2828	209.3479 9572	50

TABLE 111 - AMOUNT OF 1 PER PERIOD
How $1 deposited periodically will grow

n	2½%	3%	3½%	4%	4½%	5%	n
51	100.9214 5751	117.1807 7331	136.5828 3702	159.7737 6700	187.5356 6455	220.8153 9550	51
52	104.4444 9395	121.6961 9651	142.3632 3631	167.1647 1768	196.9747 6946	232.8561 6528	52
53	108.0556 0629	126.3470 8240	148.3459 4958	174.8513 0639	206.8386 3408	245.4989 7354	53
54	111.7569 9645	131.1374 9488	154.5380 5782	182.8453 5865	217.1463 7262	258.7739 2222	54
55	115.5509 2136	136.0716 1972	160.9468 8984	191.1591 7299	227.9179 5938	272.7126 1833	55
56	119.4396 9440	141.1537 6831	167.5800 3099	199.8055 3991	239.1742 6756	287.3482 4924	56
57	123.4256 8676	146.3883 8136	174.4453 3207	208.7977 6151	250.9371 0960	302.7156 6171	57
58	127.5113 2893	151.7800 3280	181.5509 1869	218.1496 7197	263.2292 7953	318.8514 4479	58
59	131.6991 1215	157.3334 3379	188.9052 0085	227.8756 5885	276.0745 9711	335.7940 1703	59
60	135.9915 8995	163.0534 3680	196.5168 8288	237.9906 8520	289.4979 5398	353.5837 1788	60
61	140.3913 7970	168.9450 3991	204.3949 7378	248.5103 1261	303.5253 6190	372.2629 0378	61
62	144.9011 6419	175.0133 9110	212.5487 9786	259.4507 2511	318.1840 0319	391.8760 4897	62
63	149.5236 9330	181.2637 9284	220.9880 0579	270.8287 5412	333.5022 8333	412.4698 5141	63
64	154.2617 8563	187.7017 0662	229.7225 8599	282.6619 0428	349.5098 8608	434.0933 4398	64
65	159.1183 3027	194.3327 5782	238.7628 7650	294.9683 8045	366.2378 3096	456.7980 1118	65
66	164.0962 8853	201.1627 4055	248.1195 7718	307.7671 1567	383.7185 3335	480.6379 1174	66
67	169.1986 9574	208.1976 2277	257.8037 6238	321.0778 0030	401.9858 6735	505.6698 0733	67
68	174.4286 6314	215.4435 5145	267.8268 9406	334.9209 1231	421.0752 3138	531.9532 9770	68
69	179.7893 7971	222.9068 5800	278.2008 3535	349.3177 4880	441.0236 1679	559.5509 6258	69
70	185.2841 1421	230.5940 6374	288.9378 6459	364.2904 5876	461.8696 7955	588.5285 1071	70
71	190.9162 1706	238.5118 8565	300.0506 8985	379.8620 7711	483.6538 1513	618.9549 3625	71
72	196.6891 2249	246.6672 4222	311.5524 6400	396.0565 6019	506.4182 3681	650.9026 8306	72
73	202.6063 5055	255.0672 5949	323.4568 0024	412.8988 2260	530.2070 5747	684.4478 1721	73
74	208.6715 0931	263.7192 7727	335.7777 8824	430.4147 7550	555.0663 7505	719.6702 0807	74
75	214.8882 9705	272.6308 5559	348.5300 1083	448.6313 6652	581.0443 6193	756.6537 1848	75
76	221.2605 0447	281.8097 8126	361.7285 6121	467.5766 2118	608.1913 5822	795.4864 0440	76
77	227.7920 1709	291.2640 7469	375.3890 6085	487.2796 8603	636.5599 6934	836.2607 2462	77
78	234.4868 1751	301.0019 9693	389.5276 7798	507.7708 7347	666.2051 6796	879.0737 6085	78
79	241.3489 8795	311.0320 5684	404.1611 4671	529.0817 0841	697.1844 0052	924.0274 4889	79
80	248.3827 1265	321.3630 1855	419.3067 8685	551.2449 7675	729.5576 9854	971.2288 2134	80
81	255.5922 8047	332.0039 0910	434.9825 2439	574.2947 7582	763.3877 9497	1020.7902 6240	81
82	262.9820 8748	342.9640 2638	451.2069 1274	598.2665 6685	798.7402 4575	1072.8297 7552	82
83	270.5566 3966	354.2529 4717	467.9991 5469	623.1972 2952	835.6835 5680	1127.4712 6430	83
84	278.3205 5566	365.8805 3558	485.3791 2510	649.1251 1870	874.2893 1686	1184.8448 2752	84
85	286.2785 6955	377.8569 5165	503.3673 9448	676.0901 2345	914.6323 3612	1245.0870 6889	85
86	294.4355 3379	390.1926 6020	521.9852 5329	704.1337 2839	956.7907 9125	1308.3414 2234	86
87	302.7964 2213	402.8984 4001	541.2547 3715	733.2990 7753	1000.8463 7685	1374.7584 9345	87
88	311.3663 3268	415.9853 9321	561.1986 5295	763.6310 4063	1046.8844 6381	1444.4964 1812	88
89	320.1504 9100	429.4649 5500	581.8406 0581	795.1762 8225	1094.9942 6468	1517.7212 3903	89
90	329.1542 5328	443.3489 0365	603.2050 2701	827.9833 3354	1145.2690 0659	1594.6073 0098	90
91	338.3831 0961	457.6493 7076	625.3172 0295	862.1026 6688	1197.8061 1189	1675.3376 6603	91
92	347.8426 8735	472.3788 5189	648.2033 0506	897.5867 7356	1252.7073 8692	1760.1045 4933	92
93	357.5387 5453	487.5502 1744	671.8904 2073	934.4902 4450	1310.0792 1933	1849.1097 7680	93
94	367.4772 2339	503.1767 2397	696.4065 8546	972.8698 5428	1370.0327 8420	1942.5652 6564	94
95	377.6641 5398	519.2720 2568	721.7808 1595	1012.7846 4845	1432.6842 5949	2040.6935 2892	95
96	388.1057 5783	535.8501 8645	748.0431 4451	1054.2960 3439	1498.1550 5117	2143.7282 0537	96
97	398.8084 0177	552.9256 9205	775.2246 5457	1097.4678 7577	1566.5720 2847	2251.9146 1564	97
98	409.7786 1182	570.5134 6281	803.3575 1748	1142.3665 9080	1638.0677 6976	2365.5103 4642	98
99	421.0230 7711	588.6288 6669	832.4750 3059	1189.0612 5443	1712.7808 1939	2484.7858 6374	99
100	432.5486 5404	607.2877 3270	862.6116 5666	1237.6237 0461	1790.8559 5627	2610.0251 5693	100

157

TABLE 111 - AMOUNT OF 1 PER PERIOD
How $1 deposited periodically will grow

n	5½%	6%	6½%	7%	7½%	8%	n
1	1.0000 0000	1.0000 0000	1.0000 0000	1.0000 0000	1.0000 0000	1.0000 0000	1
2	2.0550 0000	2.0600 0000	2.0650 0000	2.0700 0000	2.0750 0000	2.0800 0000	2
3	3.1680 2500	3.1836 0000	3.1992 2500	3.2149 0000	3.2306 2500	3.2464 0000	3
4	4.3422 6638	4.3746 1600	4.4071 7463	4.4399 4300	4.4729 2188	4.5061 1200	4
5	5.5810 9103	5.6370 9296	5.6936 4098	5.7507 3901	5.8083 9102	5.8666 0096	5
6	6.8880 5103	6.9753 1854	7.0637 2764	7.1532 9074	7.2440 2034	7.3359 2904	6
7	8.2668 9384	8.3938 3765	8.5228 6994	8.6540 2109	8.7873 2187	8.9228 0336	7
8	9.7215 7300	9.8974 6791	10.0768 5648	10.2598 0257	10.4463 7101	10.6366 2763	8
9	11.2562 5951	11.4913 1598	11.7318 5215	11.9779 8875	12.2298 4883	12.4875 5784	9
10	12.8753 5379	13.1807 9494	13.4944 2254	13.8164 4796	14.1470 8750	14.4865 6247	10
11	14.5834 9825	14.9716 4264	15.3715 6001	15.7835 9932	16.2081 1906	16.6454 8746	11
12	16.3855 9065	16.8699 4120	17.3707 1141	17.8884 5127	18.4237 2799	18.9771 2646	12
13	18.2867 9814	18.8821 3767	19.4998 0765	20.1406 4286	20.8055 0759	21.4952 9658	13
14	20.2925 7203	21.0150 6593	21.7672 9515	22.5504 8786	23.3659 2066	24.2149 2030	14
15	22.4086 6350	23.2759 6988	24.1821 6933	25.1290 2201	26.1183 6470	27.1521 1393	15
16	24.6411 3999	25.6725 2808	26.7540 1034	27.8880 5355	29.0772 4206	30.3242 8304	16
17	26.9964 0269	28.2128 7976	29.4930 2101	30.8402 1730	32.2580 3521	33.7502 2569	17
18	29.4812 0483	30.9056 5255	32.4100 6738	33.9990 3251	35.6773 8785	37.4502 4374	18
19	32.1026 7110	33.7599 9170	35.5167 2176	37.3789 6479	39.3531 9194	41.4462 6324	19
20	34.8683 1801	36.7855 9120	38.8253 0867	40.9954 9232	43.3046 8134	45.7619 6430	20
21	37.7860 7550	39.9927 2668	42.3489 5373	44.8651 7678	47.5525 3244	50.4229 2144	21
22	40.8643 0965	43.3922 9028	46.1016 3573	49.0057 3916	52.1189 7237	55.4567 5516	22
23	44.1118 4669	46.9958 2769	50.0982 4205	53.4361 4090	57.0278 9530	60.8932 9557	23
24	47.5379 9825	50.8155 7735	54.3546 2778	58.1766 7076	62.3049 8744	66.7647 5922	24
25	51.1525 8816	54.8645 1200	58.8876 7859	63.2490 3772	67.9778 6150	73.1059 3995	25
26	54.9659 8051	59.1563 8272	63.7153 7769	68.6764 7036	74.0762 0112	79.9544 1515	26
27	58.9891 0943	63.7057 6568	68.8568 7725	74.4838 2328	80.6319 1620	87.3507 6836	27
28	63.2335 1045	68.5281 1162	74.3325 7427	80.6976 9091	87.6793 0991	95.3388 2983	28
29	67.7113 5353	73.6397 9832	80.1641 9159	87.3465 2927	95.2552 5816	103.9659 3622	29
30	72.4354 7797	79.0581 8622	86.3748 6405	94.4607 8632	103.3994 0252	113.2832 1111	30
31	77.4194 2926	84.8016 7739	92.9892 3021	102.0730 4137	112.1543 5771	123.3458 6800	31
32	82.6774 9787	90.8897 7803	100.0335 3017	110.2181 5426	121.5659 3454	134.2135 3744	32
33	88.2247 6025	97.3431 6471	107.5357 0963	118.9334 2506	131.6833 7963	145.9506 2044	33
34	94.0771 2207	104.1837 5460	115.5255 3076	128.2587 6481	142.5596 3310	158.6266 7007	34
35	100.2513 6378	111.4347 7987	124.0346 9026	138.2368 7835	154.2516 0558	172.3168 0368	35
36	106.7651 8879	119.1208 6666	133.0969 4513	148.9134 5984	166.8204 7600	187.1021 4797	36
37	113.6372 7417	127.2681 1866	142.7482 4656	160.3374 0202	180.3320 1170	203.0703 1981	37
38	120.8873 2425	135.9042 0578	153.0268 8259	172.5610 2017	194.8569 1258	220.3159 4540	38
39	128.5361 2708	145.0584 5813	163.9736 2996	185.6402 9158	210.4711 8102	238.9412 2103	39
40	136.6056 1407	154.7619 6562	175.6319 1590	199.6351 1199	227.2565 1960	259.0565 1871	40
41	145.1189 2285	165.0476 8356	188.0479 9044	214.6095 6983	245.3007 5857	280.7810.4021	41
42	154.1004 6360	175.9505 4457	201.2711 0981	230.6322 3972	264.6983 1546	304.2435 2342	42
43	163.5759 8910	187.5075 7724	215.3537 3195	247.7764 9650	285.5506 8912	329.5830 0530	43
44	173.5726 6850	199.7580 3188	230.3517 2453	266.1208 5125	307.9669 9080	356.9496 4572	44
45	184.1191 6527	212.7435 1379	246.3245 8662	285.7493 1084	332.0645 1511	386.5056 1738	45
46	195.2457 1936	226.5081 2462	263.3356 8475	306.7517 6260	357.9693 5375	418.4260 6677	46
47	206.9842 3392	241.0986 1210	281.4525 0426	329.2243 8598	385.8170 5528	452.9001 5211	47
48	219.3683 6679	256.5645 2882	300.7469 1704	353.2700 9300	415.7533 3442	490.1321 6428	48
49	232.4336 2696	272.9584 0055	321.2954 6665	378.9989 9951	447.9348 3451	530.3427 3742	49
50	246.2174 7645	290.3359 0458	343.1796 7198	406.5289 2947	482.5299 4709	573.7701 5642	50

158

ANNUITIES

Now let's discuss another problem involving annuities. **Determine the periodic payment for the future amount of an annuity.** Let's ask the question, suppose I want to accumulate $500,000 in 30 years. How much must I pay myself every year to do this.

The equation is R = AC

Where A is the future amount,
 R is the periodic payment,
and C is a **constant** from the tables.

In this example A = $500,000; so the equation is:

R = $500,000 x C

To determine C, we use **TABLE IV** titled **SINKING FUND**. This table follows this discussion beginning on page 161.

[1] Determine the interest rate PER PERIOD.
In this case the PERIOD is one year. The interest rate is 8%.
[2] Turn to the tables and locate the column title 8%. (Page 168.)
[3] The column titled n stands for number of PERIODS. Move down to the number 30 and under 8% you will see the **constant** .0088 2743.
[4] Multiplying the **constant** by $500,000.00 gives the periodic payment of $4,413.72 rounded off to two decimal places.

R = AC
R = $500,000 x .0088 2743
R = $4,413.72 per year

Dividing by 12 gives a monthly payment of **$367.80 per month**. However, the interest was compounded annually. Now we will solve the same problem with the interest compounded **monthly** using tables that are not included here.

$$R = AC$$
$$R = \$500,000 \times .000\ 670\ 9791$$
$$R = \textbf{\$335.49 per month}$$

The last example will be a problem using interest compounded monthly with a period that you can determine using the TABLE IV.

How much must I pay myself per month to accumulate $100,000 in 8 years at 9% compounded **monthly**?

[1] Determine the interest rate PER PERIOD. (9% divided by 12 = 3/4%.

[2] Turn to the tables and locate the column titled 3/4%. (Page 165.)

[3] The column titled n stands for number of PERIODS. Move down to the number 96 (8 x 12 months) and see the **constant** .0071 5020.

[4] Multiplying the **constant** by $100,000.00 gives the periodic payment of $715.02 rounded off to two decimal places.

$$R = AC$$
$$R = \$100,000 \times .0071\ 5020$$
$$R = \$715.02$$

The four basic categories of problems cover everything you will need to know about the value of money and the miracle of compound interest.

TABLE IV - SINKING FUND
Periodic deposit that will grow to $1 at future date

n	$\frac{1}{4}\%$	$\frac{1}{3}\%$	$\frac{5}{12}\%$	$\frac{1}{2}\%$	$\frac{7}{12}\%$	$\frac{2}{3}\%$	n
1	1.0000 0000	1.0000 0000	1.0000 0000	1.0000 0000	1.0000 0000	1.0000 0000	1
2	0.4993 7578	0.4991 6805	0.4989 6050	0.4987 5312	0.4985 4591	0.4983 3887	2
3	0.3325 0139	0.3322 2469	0.3319 4829	0.3316 7221	0.3313 9643	0.3311 2095	3
4	0.2490 6445	0.2487 5347	0.2484 4291	0.2481 3279	0.2478 2310	0.2475 1384	4
5	0.1990 0250	0.1986 7110	0.1983 4026	0.1980 0997	0.1976 8024	0.1973 5105	5
6	0.1656 2803	0.1652 8317	0.1649 3898	0.1645 9546	0.1642 5260	0.1639 1042	6
7	0.1417 8928	0.1414 3491	0.1410 8133	0.1407 2854	0.1403 7653	0.1400 2531	7
8	0.1239 1035	0.1235 4895	0.1231 8845	0.1228 2886	0.1224 7018	0.1221 1240	8
9	0.1100 0462	0.1096 3785	0.1092 7209	0.1089 0736	0.1085 4365	0.1081 8096	9
10	0.0988 8015	0.0985 0915	0.0981 3929	0.0977 7057	0.0974 0299	0.0970 3654	10
11	0.0897 7840	0.0894 0402	0.0890 3090	0.0886 5903	0.0882 8842	0.0879 1905	11
12	0.0821 9370	0.0818 1657	0.0814 4082	0.0810 6643	0.0806 9341	0.0803 2176	12
13	0.0757 7595	0.0753 9656	0.0750 1866	0.0746 4224	0.0742 6730	0.0738 9385	13
14	0.0702 7510	0.0698 9383	0.0695 1416	0.0691 3609	0.0687 5962	0.0638 8474	14
15	0.0655 0777	0.0651 2491	0.0647 4378	0.0643 6436	0.0639 8666	0.0636 1067	15
16	0.0613 3642	0.0609 5223	0.0605 6988	0.0601 8937	0.0598 1068	0.0594 3382	16
17	0.0576 5587	0.0572 7056	0.0568 8720	0.0565 0579	0.0561 2632	0.0557 4880	17
18	0.0543 8433	0.0539 9807	0.0536 1387	0.0532 3173	0.0528 5165	0.0524 7363	18
19	0.0514 5722	0.0510 7015	0.0506 8525	0.0503 0253	0.0499 2198	0.0495 4361	19
20	0.0488 2288	0.0484 3511	0.0480 4963	0.0476 6645	0.0472 8556	0.0469 0696	20
21	0.0464 3947	0.0460 5111	0.0456 6517	0.0452 8163	0.0449 0050	0.0445 2176	21
22	0.0442 7278	0.0438 8393	0.0434 9760	0.0431 1380	0.0427 3251	0.0423 5374	22
23	0.0422 9455	0.0419 0528	0.0415 1865	0.0411 3465	0.0407 5329	0.0403 7456	23
24	0.0404 8121	0.0400 9159	0.0397 0472	0.0393 2061	0.0389 3925	0.0385 6062	24
25	0.0388 1298	0.0384 2307	0.0380 3603	0.0376 5186	0.0372 7055	0.0368 9210	25
26	0.0372 7312	0.0368 8297	0.0364 9581	0.0361 1163	0.0357 3043	0.0353 5220	26
27	0.0358 4736	0.0354 5702	0.0350 6978	0.0346 8565	0.0343 0460	0.0339 2664	27
28	0.0345 2347	0.0341 3299	0.0337 4572	0.0333 6167	0.0329 8082	0.0326 0317	28
29	0.0332 9093	0.0329 0033	0.0325 1307	0.0321 2914	0.0317 4853	0.0313 7123	29
30	0.0321 4059	0.0317 4992	0.0313 6270	0.0309 7892	0.0305 9857	0.0302 2166	30
31	0.0310 6449	0.0306 7378	0.0302 8663	0.0299 0304	0.0295 2299	0.0291 4649	31
32	0.0300 5569	0.0296 6496	0.0292 7791	0.0288 9453	0.0285 1482	0.0281 3875	32
33	0.0291 0806	0.0287 1734	0.0283 3041	0.0279 4727	0.0275 6791	0.0271 9231	33
34	0.0282 1620	0.0278 2551	0.0274 3873	0.0270 5586	0.0266 7687	0.0263 0176	34
35	0.0273 7533	0.0269 8470	0.0265 9809	0.0262 1550	0.0258 3691	0.0254 6231	35
36	0.0265 8121	0.0261 9065	0.0258 0423	0.0254 2194	0.0250 4376	0.0246 6970	36
37	0.0258 3004	0.0254 3957	0.0250 5336	0.0246 7139	0.0242 9365	0.0239 2013	37
38	0.0251 1843	0.0247 2808	0.0243 4208	0.0239 6045	0.0235 8316	0.0232 1020	38
39	0.0244 4335	0.0240 5311	0.0236 6736	0.0232 8607	0.0229 0925	0.0225 3687	39
40	0.0238 0204	0.0234 1194	0.0230 2644	0.0226 4552	0.0222 6917	0.0218 9739	40
41	0.0231 9204	0.0228 0209	0.0224 1685	0.0220 3631	0.0216 6046	0.0212 8928	41
42	0.0226 1112	0.0222 2133	0.0218 3637	0.0214 5622	0.0210 8087	0.0207 1031	42
43	0.0220 5724	0.0216 6762	0.0212 8295	0.0209 0320	0.0205 2836	0.0201 5843	43
44	0.0215 2855	0.0211 3912	0.0207 5474	0.0203 7541	0.0200 0110	0.0196 3180	44
45	0.0210 2339	0.0206 3415	0.0202 5008	0.0198 7117	0.0194 9740	0.0191 2875	45
46	0.0205 4022	0.0201 5118	0.0197 6743	0.0193 8894	0.0190 1571	0.0186 4772	46
47	0.0200 7762	0.0196 8880	0.0193 0537	0.0189 2733	0.0185 5465	0.0181 8732	47
48	0.0196 3433	0.0192 4572	0.0188 6263	0.0184 8503	0.0181 1291	0.0177 4626	48
49	0.0192 0915	0.0188 2077	0.0184 3801	0.0180 6087	0.0176 8932	0.0173 2334	49
50	0.0188 0099	0.0184 1285	0.0180 3044	0.0176 5376	0.0172 8278	0.0169 1749	50

TABLE IV - SINKING FUND
Periodic deposit that will grow to $1 at future date

n	$\frac{1}{4}\%$	$\frac{1}{3}\%$	$\frac{5}{12}\%$	$\frac{1}{2}\%$	$\frac{7}{12}\%$	$\frac{2}{3}\%$	n
51	0.0184 0886	0.0180 2096	0.0176 3891	0.0172 6269	0.0168 9230	0.0165 2770	51
52	0.0180 3184	0.0176 4418	0.0172 6249	0.0168 8675	0.0165 1694	0.0161 5304	52
53	0.0176 6906	0.0172 8165	0.0169 0033	0.0165 2507	0.0161 5585	0.0157 9266	53
54	0.0173 1974	0.0169 3259	0.0165 5164	0.0161 7686	0.0158 0824	0.0154 4576	54
55	0.0169 8314	0.0165 9625	0.0162 1567	0.0158 4139	0.0154 7337	0.0151 1160	55
56	0.0166 5858	0.0162 7196	0.0158 9176	0.0155 1797	0.0151 5056	0.0147 8951	56
57	0.0163 4542	0.0159 5907	0.0155 7927	0.0152 0598	0.0148 3918	0.0144 7885	57
58	0.0160 4308	0.0156 5701	0.0152 7760	0.0149 0481	0.0145 3863	0.0141 7903	58
59	0.0157 5101	0.0153 6522	0.0149 8620	0.0146 1392	0.0142 4836	0.0138 8949	59
60	0.0154 6869	0.0150 8319	0.0147 0457	0.0143 3280	0.0139 6787	0.0136 0973	60
61	0.0151 9564	0.0148 1043	0.0144 3221	0.0140 6096	0.0136 9666	0.0133 3926	61
62	0.0149 3142	0.0145 4650	0.0141 6869	0.0137 9796	0.0134 3428	0.0130 7763	62
63	0.0146 7561	0.0142 9098	0.0139 1358	0.0135 4337	0.0131 8033	0.0128 2442	63
64	0.0144 2780	0.0140 4348	0.0136 6649	0.0132 9681	0.0129 3440	0.0125 7923	64
65	0.0141 8764	0.0138 0361	0.0134 2704	0.0130 5789	0.0126 9612	0.0123 4171	65
66	0.0139 5476	0.0135 7105	0.0131 9489	0.0128 2627	0.0124 6515	0.0121 1149	66
67	0.0137 2886	0.0133 4545	0.0129 6972	0.0126 0163	0.0122 4116	0.0118 8825	67
68	0.0135 0961	0.0131 2652	0.0127 5121	0.0123 8366	0.0120 2383	0.0116 7168	68
69	0.0132 9674	0.0129 1395	0.0125 3908	0.0121 7206	0.0118 1289	0.0114 6150	69
70	0.0130 8996	0.0127 0749	0.0123 3304	0.0119 6657	0.0116 0805	0.0112 5742	70
71	0.0128 8902	0.0125 0687	0.0121 3285	0.0117 6693	0.0114 0906	0.0110 5919	71
72	0.0126 9368	0.0123 1185	0.0119 3827	0.0115 7289	0.0112 1567	0.0108 6657	72
73	0.0125 0370	0.0121 2220	0.0117 4905	0.0113 8422	0.0110 2766	0.0106 7933	73
74	0.0123 1887	0.0119 3769	0.0115 6498	0.0112 0070	0.0108 4481	0.0104 9725	74
75	0.0121 3898	0.0117 5813	0.0113 8586	0.0110 2214	0.0106 6690	0.0103 2011	75
76	0.0119 6385	0.0115 8332	0.0112 1150	0.0108 4832	0.0104 9375	0.0101 4773	76
77	0.0117 9327	0.0114 1308	0.0110 4170	0.0106 7908	0.0103 2517	0.0099 7993	77
78	0.0116 2708	0.0112 4722	0.0108 7629	0.0105 1423	0.0101 6099	0.0098 1652	78
79	0.0114 6511	0.0110 8559	0.0107 1510	0.0103 5360	0.0100 0103	0.0096 5733	79
80	0.0113 0721	0.0109 2802	0.0105 5798	0.0101 9704	0.0098 4514	0.0095 0222	80
81	0.0111 5321	0.0107 7436	0.0104 0477	0.0100 4439	0.0096 9316	0.0093 5102	81
82	0.0110 0298	0.0106 2447	0.0102 5534	0.0098 9552	0.0095 4496	0.0092 0360	82
83	0.0108 5639	0.0104 7822	0.0101 0954	0.0097 5028	0.0094 0040	0.0090 5982	83
84	0.0107 1330	0.0103 3547	0.0099 6724	0.0096 0855	0.0092 5935	0.0089 1955	84
85	0.0105 7359	0.0101 9610	0.0098 2833	0.0094 7021	0.0091 2168	0.0087 8266	85
86	0.0104 3714	0.0100 6000	0.0096 9268	0.0093 3513	0.0089 8727	0.0086 4904	86
87	0.0103 0384	0.0099 2704	0.0095 6018	0.0092 0320	0.0088 5602	0.0085 1857	87
88	0.0101 7357	0.0097 9713	0.0094 3073	0.0090 7431	0.0087 2781	0.0083 9115	88
89	0.0100 4625	0.0096 7015	0.0093 0422	0.0089 4837	0.0086 0255	0.0082 6667	89
90	0.0099 2177	0.0095 4602	0.0091 8055	0.0088 2527	0.0084 8013	0.0081 4504	90
91	0.0098 0004	0.0094 2464	0.0090 5962	0.0087 0493	0.0083 6047	0.0080 2616	91
92	0.0096 8096	0.0093 0592	0.0089 4136	0.0085 8724	0.0082 4346	0.0079 0994	92
93	0.0095 6446	0.0091 8976	0.0088 2568	0.0084 7213	0.0081 2903	0.0077 9629	93
94	0.0094 5044	0.0090 7610	0.0087 1248	0.0083 5950	0.0080 1709	0.0076 8514	94
95	0.0093 3884	0.0089 6485	0.0086 0170	0.0082 4930	0.0079 0757	0.0075 7641	95
96	0.0092 2957	0.0088 5594	0.0084 9325	0.0081 4143	0.0078 0038	0.0074 7001	96
97	0.0091 2257	0.0087 4929	0.0083 8707	0.0080 3583	0.0076 9547	0.0073 6588	97
98	0.0090 1776	0.0086 4484	0.0082 8309	0.0079 3242	0.0075 9275	0.0072 6394	98
99	0.0089 1508	0.0085 4252	0.0081 8124	0.0078 3115	0.0074 9216	0.0071 6415	99
100	0.0088 1446	0.0084 4226	0.0080 8145	0.0077 3194	0.0073 9363	0.0070 6642	100

162

TABLE IV - SINKING FUND
Periodic deposit that will grow to $1 at future date

n	$\frac{1}{4}\%$	$\frac{1}{3}\%$	$\frac{5}{12}\%$	$\frac{1}{2}\%$	$\frac{7}{12}\%$	$\frac{2}{3}\%$	n
101	0.0087 1584	0.0083 4400	0.0079 8366	0.0076 3473	0.0072 9711	0.0069 7069	101
102	0.0086 1917	0.0082 4769	0.0078 8782	0.0075 3947	0.0072 0254	0.0068 7690	102
103	0.0085 2439	0.0081 5327	0.0077 9387	0.0074 4610	0.0071 0986	0.0067 8501	103
104	0.0084 3144	0.0080 6068	0.0077 0175	0.0073 5457	0.0070 1901	0.0066 9495	104
105	0.0083 4027	0.0079 6987	0.0076 1142	0.0072 6481	0.0069 2994	0.0066 0668	105
106	0.0082 5082	0.0078 8079	0.0075 2281	0.0071 7679	0.0068 4261	0.0065 2013	106
107	0.0081 6307	0.0077 9340	0.0074 3589	0.0070 9045	0.0067 5696	0.0064 3527	107
108	0.0080 7694	0.0077 0764	0.0073 5061	0.0070 0575	0.0066 7294	0.0063 5205	108
109	0.0079 9241	0.0076 2347	0.0072 6691	0.0069 2264	0.0065 9052	0.0062 7042	109
110	0.0079 0942	0.0075 4084	0.0071 8476	0.0068 4107	0.0065 0965	0.0061 9033	110
111	0.0078 2793	0.0074 5972	0.0071 0412	0.0067 6102	0.0064 3028	0.0061 1175	111
112	0.0077 4791	0.0073 8007	0.0070 2495	0.0066 8242	0.0063 5237	0.0060 3464	112
113	0.0076 6932	0.0073 0184	0.0069 4720	0.0066 0526	0.0062 7590	0.0059 5895	113
114	0.0075 9211	0.0072 2500	0.0068 7083	0.0065 2948	0.0062 0081	0.0058 8465	114
115	0.0075 1626	0.0071 4952	0.0067 9582	0.0064 5506	0.0061 2708	0.0058 1171	115
116	0.0074 4172	0.0070 7535	0.0067 2213	0.0063 8195	0.0060 5466	0.0057 4008	116
117	0.0073 6846	0.0070 0246	0.0066 4973	0.0063 1013	0.0059 8353	0.0056 6974	117
118	0.0072 9646	0.0069 3082	0.0065 7857	0.0062 3956	0.0059 1365	0.0056 0065	118
119	0.0072 2567	0.0068 6041	0.0065 0863	0.0061 7021	0.0058 4499	0.0055 3278	119
120	0.0071 5607	0.0067 9118	0.0064 3988	0.0061 0205	0.0057 7751	0.0054 6609	120
121	0.0070 8764	0.0067 2311	0.0063 7230	0.0060 3505	0.0057 1120	0.0054 0057	121
122	0.0070 2033	0.0066 5617	0.0063 0584	0.0059 6918	0.0056 4602	0.0053 3618	122
123	0.0069 5412	0.0065 9034	0.0062 4049	0.0059 0441	0.0055 8194	0.0052 7289	123
124	0.0068 8899	0.0065 2558	0.0061 7621	0.0058 4072	0.0055 1894	0.0052 1067	124
125	0.0068 2491	0.0064 6188	0.0061 1298	0.0057 7808	0.0054 5700	0.0051 4951	125
126	0.0067 6186	0.0063 9919	0.0060 5078	0.0057 1647	0.0053 9607	0.0050 8937	126
127	0.0066 9981	0.0063 3751	0.0059 8959	0.0056 5586	0.0053 3615	0.0050 3024	127
128	0.0066 3873	0.0062 7681	0.0059 2937	0.0055 9623	0.0052 7721	0.0049 7208	128
129	0.0065 7861	0.0062 1707	0.0058 7010	0.0055 3755	0.0052 1922	0.0049 1488	129
130	0.0065 1942	0.0061 5825	0.0058 1177	0.0054 7981	0.0051 6216	0.0048 5861	130
131	0.0064 6115	0.0061 0035	0.0057 5435	0.0054 2298	0.0051 0602	0.0048 0325	131
132	0.0064 0376	0.0060 4334	0.0056 9782	0.0053 6703	0.0050 5077	0.0047 4878	132
133	0.0063 4725	0.0059 8720	0.0056 4216	0.0053 1197	0.0049 9639	0.0046 9518	133
134	0.0062 9159	0.0059 3191	0.0055 8736	0.0052 5775	0.0049 4286	0.0046 4244	134
135	0.0062 3675	0.0058 7745	0.0055 3339	0.0052 0436	0.0048 9016	0.0045 9052	135
136	0.0061 8274	0.0058 2381	0.0054 8023	0.0051 5179	0.0048 3828	0.0045 3942	136
137	0.0061 2952	0.0057 7097	0.0054 2787	0.0051 0002	0.0047 8719	0.0044 8911	137
138	0.0060 7707	0.0057 1890	0.0053 7628	0.0050 4902	0.0047 3688	0.0044 3959	138
139	0.0060 2539	0.0056 6760	0.0053 2546	0.0049 9879	0.0046 8733	0.0043 9082	139
140	0.0059 7446	0.0056 1704	0.0052 7539	0.0049 4930	0.0046 3853	0.0043 4280	140
141	0.0059 2425	0.0055 6721	0.0052 2604	0.0049 0055	0.0045 9046	0.0042 9551	141
142	0.0058 7476	0.0055 1809	0.0051 7741	0.0048 5250	0.0045 4311	0.0042 4893	142
143	0.0058 2597	0.0054 6968	0.0051 2948	0.0048 0516	0.0044 9645	0.0042 0305	143
144	0.0057 7787	0.0054 2195	0.0050 8224	0.0047 5850	0.0044 5048	0.0041 5786	144
145	0.0057 3043	0.0053 7489	0.0050 3566	0.0047 1252	0.0044 0518	0.0041 1333	145
146	0.0056 8365	0.0053 2849	0.0049 8975	0.0046 6718	0.0043 6053	0.0040 6947	146
147	0.0056 3752	0.0052 8273	0.0049 4447	0.0046 2250	0.0043 1653	0.0040 2624	147
148	0.0055 9201	0.0052 3760	0.0048 9983	0.0045 7844	0.0042 7316	0.0039 8364	148
149	0.0055 4712	0.0051 9309	0.0048 5580	0.0045 3500	0.0042 3040	0.0039 4166	149
150	0.0055 0284	0.0051 4919	0.0048 1238	0.0044 9217	0.0041 8825	0.0039 0029	150

163

TABLE IV - SINKING FUND
TABLE IV - SINKING FUND
Periodic deposit that will grow to $1 at future date

n	$\frac{3}{4}\%$	1%	$1\frac{1}{4}\%$	$1\frac{1}{2}\%$	$1\frac{3}{4}\%$	2%	n
1	1.0000 0000	1.0000 0000	1.0000 0000	1.0000 0000	1.0000 0000	1.0000 0000	1
2	0.4981 3200	0.4975 1244	0.4968 9441	0.4962 7792	0.4956 6295	0.4950 4950	2
3	0.3308 4579	0.3300 2211	0.3292 0117	0.3283 8296	0.3275 6746	0.3267 5467	3
4	0.2472 0501	0.2462 8109	0.2453 6102	0.2444 4479	0.2435 3237	0.2426 2375	4
5	0.1970 2242	0.1960 3980	0.1950 6211	0.1940 8932	0.1931 2142	0.1921 5839	5
6	0.1635 6891	0.1625 4837	0.1615 3381	0.1605 2521	0.1595 2256	0.1585 2581	6
7	0.1396 7488	0.1386 2828	0.1375 8872	0.1365 5616	0.1355 3059	0.1345 1196	7
8	0.1217 5552	0.1206 9029	0.1196 3314	0.1185 8402	0.1175 4292	0.1165 0980	8
9	0.1078 1929	0.1067 4036	0.1056 7055	0.1046 0982	0.1035 5813	0.1025 1544	9
10	0.0966 7123	0.0955 8208	0.0945 0307	0.0934 3418	0.0923 7534	0.0913 2653	10
11	0.0875 5094	0.0864 5408	0.0853 6839	0.0842 9384	0.0832 3038	0.0821 7794	11
12	0.0799 5148	0.0788 4879	0.0777 5831	0.0766 7999	0.0756 1377	0.0745 5960	12
13	0.0735 2188	0.0724 1482	0.0713 2100	0.0702 4036	0.0691 7283	0.0681 1835	13
14	0.0680 1146	0.0669 0117	0.0658 0515	0.0647 2332	0.0636 5562	0.0626 0197	14
15	0.0632 3639	0.0621 2378	0.0610 2646	0.0599 4436	0.0588 7739	0.0578 2547	15
16	0.0590 5879	0.0579 4460	0.0568 4672	0.0557 6508	0.0546 9958	0.0536 5013	16
17	0.0553 7321	0.0542 5806	0.0531 6023	0.0520 7966	0.0510 1623	0.0499 6984	17
18	0.0520 9766	0.0509 8205	0.0498 8479	0.0488 0578	0.0477 4492	0.0467 0210	18
19	0.0491 6740	0.0480 5175	0.0469 5548	0.0458 7847	0.0448 2061	0.0437 8177	19
20	0.0465 3063	0.0454 1531	0.0443 2039	0.0432 4574	0.0421 9122	0.0411 5672	20
21	0.0441 4543	0.0430 3075	0.0419 3749	0.0408 6550	0.0398 1464	0.0387 8477	21
22	0.0419 7748	0.0408 6372	0.0397 7238	0.0387 0332	0.0376 5638	0.0366 3140	22
23	0.0399 9846	0.0388 8584	0.0377 9666	0.0367 3075	0.0356 8796	0.0346 6810	23
24	0.0381 8474	0.0370 7347	0.0359 8665	0.0349 2410	0.0338 8565	0.0328 7110	24
25	0.0365 1650	0.0354 0675	0.0343 2247	0.0332 6345	0.0322 2952	0.0312 2044	25
26	0.0349 7693	0.0338 6888	0.0327 8729	0.0317 3196	0.0307 0269	0.0296 9923	26
27	0.0335 5176	0.0324 4553	0.0313 6677	0.0303 1527	0.0292 9079	0.0282 9309	27
28	0.0322 2871	0.0311 2444	0.0300 4863	0.0290 0108	0.0279 8151	0.0269 8967	28
29	0.0309 9723	0.0298 9502	0.0288 2228	0.0277 7878	0.0267 6424	0.0257 7836	29
30	0.0298 4816	0.0287 4811	0.0276 7854	0.0266 3919	0.0256 2975	0.0246 4992	30
31	0.0287 7352	0.0276 7573	0.0266 0942	0.0255 7430	0.0245 7005	0.0235 9635	31
32	0.0277 6634	0.0266 7089	0.0256 0791	0.0245 7710	0.0235 7812	0.0226 1061	32
33	0.0268 2048	0.0257 2744	0.0246 6786	0.0236 4144	0.0226 4779	0.0216 8653	33
34	0.0259 3053	0.0248 3997	0.0237 8387	0.0227 6189	0.0217 7363	0.0208 1867	34
35	0.0250 9170	0.0240 0368	0.0229 5111	0.0219 3363	0.0209 5082	0.0200 0221	35
36	0.0242 9973	0.0232 1431	0.0221 6533	0.0211 5240	0.0201 7507	0.0192 3285	36
37	0.0235 5082	0.0224 6805	0.0214 2270	0.0204 1437	0.0194 4257	0.0185 0678	37
38	0.0228 4157	0.0217 6150	0.0207 1983	0.0197 1613	0.0187 4990	0.0178 2057	38
39	0.0221 6893	0.0210 9160	0.0200 5365	0.0190 5463	0.0180 9399	0.0171 7114	39
40	0.0215 3016	0.0204 5560	0.0194 2141	0.0184 2710	0.0174 7209	0.0165 5575	40
41	0.0209 2276	0.0198 5102	0.0188 2063	0.0178 3106	0.0168 8170	0.0159 7188	41
42	0.0203 4452	0.0192 7563	0.0182 4906	0.0172 6426	0.0163 2057	0.0154 1729	42
43	0.0197 9338	0.0187 2737	0.0177 0466	0.0167 2465	0.0157 8666	0.0148 8993	43
44	0.0192 6751	0.0182 0441	0.0171 8557	0.0162 1038	0.0152 7810	0.0143 8794	44
45	0.0187 6521	0.0177 0505	0.0166 9012	0.0157 1976	0.0147 9321	0.0139 0962	45
46	0.0182 8495	0.0172 2775	0.0162 1675	0.0152 5125	0.0143 3043	0.0134 5342	46
47	0.0178 2532	0.0167 7111	0.0157 6406	0.0148 0342	0.0138 8836	0.0130 1792	47
48	0.0173 8504	0.0163 3384	0.0153 3075	0.0143 7500	0.0134 6569	0.0126 0184	48
49	0.0169 6292	0.0159 1474	0.0149 1563	0.0139 6478	0.0130 6124	0.0122 0396	49
50	0.0165 5787	0.0155 1273	0.0145 1763	0.0135 7168	0.0126 7391	0.0118 2321	50

TABLE IV - SINKING FUND
Periodic deposit that will grow to $1 at future date

n	$\frac{3}{4}\%$	1%	$1\frac{1}{4}\%$	$1\frac{1}{2}\%$	$1\frac{3}{4}\%$	2%	n
51	0.0161 6888	0.0151 2680	0.0141 3571	0.0131 9469	0.0123 0269	0.0114 5856	51
52	0.0157 9503	0.0147 5603	0.0137 6897	0.0128 3287	0.0119 4665	0.0111 0909	52
53	0.0154 3546	0.0143 9956	0.0134 1653	0.0124 8537	0.0116 0492	0.0107 7392	53
54	0.0150 8938	0.0140 5658	0.0130 7760	0.0121 5138	0.0112 7672	0.0104 5226	54
55	0.0147 5605	0.0137 2637	0.0127 5145	0.0118 3018	0.0109 6129	0.0101 4337	55
56	0.0144 3478	0.0134 0824	0.0124 3739	0.0115 2106	0.0106 5795	0.0098 4656	56
57	0.0141 2496	0.0131 0156	0.0121 3478	0.0112 2341	0.0103 6606	0.0095 6120	57
58	0.0138 2597	0.0128 0573	0.0118 4303	0.0109 3661	0.0100 8503	0.0092 8667	58
59	0.0135 3727	0.0125 2020	0.0115 6158	0.0106 6012	0.0098 1430	0.0090 2243	59
60	0.0132 5836	0.0122 4445	0.0112 8993	0.0103 9343	0.0095 5336	0.0087 6797	60
61	0.0129 8873	0.0119 7800	0.0110 2758	0.0101 3604	0.0093 0172	0.0085 2278	61
62	0.0127 2795	0.0117 2041	0.0107 7410	0.0098 8751	0.0090 5892	0.0082 8643	62
63	0.0124 7560	0.0114 7125	0.0105 2904	0.0096 4741	0.0088 2455	0.0080 5848	63
64	0.0122 3127	0.0112 3013	0.0102 9203	0.0094 1534	0.0085 9821	0.0078 3855	64
65	0.0119 9460	0.0109 9667	0.0100 6268	0.0091 9094	0.0083 7952	0.0076 2624	65
66	0.0117 6524	0.0107 7052	0.0098 4065	0.0089 7386	0.0081 6813	0.0074 2122	66
67	0.0115 4286	0.0105 5136	0.0096 2560	0.0087 6376	0.0079 6372	0.0072 2316	67
68	0.0113 2716	0.0103 3889	0.0094 1724	0.0085 6033	0.0077 6597	0.0070 3173	68
69	0.0111 1785	0.0101 3280	0.0092 1527	0.0083 6329	0.0075 7459	0.0068 4665	69
70	0.0109 1464	0.0099 3282	0.0090 1941	0.0081 7235	0.0073 8930	0.0066 6765	70
71	0.0107 1728	0.0097 3870	0.0088 2941	0.0079 8727	0.0072 0985	0.0064 9446	71
72	0.0105 2554	0.0095 5019	0.0086 4501	0.0078 0779	0.0070 3600	0.0063 2683	72
73	0.0103 3917	0.0093 6706	0.0084 6600	0.0076 3368	0.0068 6750	0.0061 6454	73
74	0.0101 5796	0.0091 8910	0.0082 9215	0.0074 6473	0.0067 0413	0.0060 0736	74
75	0.0099 8170	0.0090 1609	0.0081 2325	0.0073 0072	0.0065 4570	0.0058 5508	75
76	0.0098 1020	0.0088 4784	0.0079 5910	0.0071 4146	0.0063 9200	0.0057 0751	76
77	0.0096 4328	0.0086 8416	0.0077 9953	0.0069 8676	0.0062 4285	0.0055 6447	77
78	0.0094 8074	0.0085 2488	0.0076 4436	0.0068 3645	0.0060 9806	0.0054 2576	78
79	0.0093 2244	0.0083 6983	0.0074 9341	0.0066 9036	0.0059 5748	0.0052 9123	79
80	0.0091 6821	0.0082 1885	0.0073 4652	0.0065 4832	0.0058 2093	0.0051 6071	80
81	0.0090 1790	0.0080 7179	0.0072 0356	0.0064 1019	0.0056 8828	0.0050 3405	81
82	0.0088 7136	0.0079 2851	0.0070 6437	0.0062 7583	0.0055 5936	0.0049 1110	82
83	0.0087 2847	0.0077 8887	0.0069 2881	0.0061 4509	0.0054 3406	0.0047 9173	83
84	0.0085 8908	0.0076 5273	0.0067 9675	0.0060 1784	0.0053 1223	0.0046 7581	84
85	0.0084 5308	0.0075 1998	0.0066 6808	0.0058 9396	0.0051 9375	0.0045 6321	85
86	0.0083 2034	0.0073 9050	0.0065 4267	0.0057 7333	0.0050 7850	0.0044 5381	86
87	0.0081 9076	0.0072 6418	0.0064 2041	0.0056 5584	0.0049 6636	0.0043 4750	87
88	0.0080 6423	0.0071 4089	0.0063 0119	0.0055 4138	0.0048 5724	0.0042 4416	88
89	0.0079 4064	0.0070 2056	0.0061 8491	0.0054 2984	0.0047 5102	0.0041 4370	89
90	0.0078 1989	0.0069 0306	0.0060 7146	0.0053 2113	0.0046 4760	0.0040 4602	90
91	0.0077 0190	0.0067 8832	0.0059 6076	0.0052 1516	0.0045 4690	0.0039 5101	91
92	0.0075 8657	0.0066 7624	0.0058 5272	0.0051 1182	0.0044 4882	0.0038 5859	92
93	0.0074 7382	0.0065 6673	0.0057 4724	0.0050 1104	0.0043 5327	0.0037 6868	93
94	0.0073 6356	0.0064 5971	0.0056 4425	0.0049 1273	0.0042 6017	0.0036 8118	94
95	0.0072 5571	0.0063 5511	0.0055 4366	0.0048 1681	0.0041 6944	0.0035 9602	95
96	0.0071 5020	0.0062 5284	0.0054 4541	0.0047 2321	0.0040 8101	0.0035 1313	96
97	0.0070 4696	0.0061 5284	0.0053 4941	0.0046 3186	0.0039 9480	0.0034 3242	97
98	0.0069 4592	0.0060 5503	0.0052 5560	0.0045 4268	0.0039 1074	0.0033 5383	98
99	0.0068 4701	0.0059 5936	0.0051 6391	0.0044 5560	0.0038 2876	0.0032 7729	99
100	0.0067 5017	0.0058 6574	0.0050 7428	0.0043 7057	0.0037 4880	0.0032 0274	100

n	$2\frac{1}{2}\%$	3%	$3\frac{1}{2}\%$	4%	$4\frac{1}{2}\%$	5%	n
1	1.0000 0000	1.0000 0000	1.0000 0000	1.0000 0000	1.0000 0000	1.0000 0000	1
2	0.4938 2716	0.4926 1084	0.4914 0049	0.4901 9608	0.4889 9756	0.4878 0488	2
3	0.3251 3717	0.3235 3036	0.3219 3418	0.3203 4854	0.3187 7336	0.3172 0856	3
4	0.2408 1788	0.2390 2705	0.2372 5114	0.2354 9005	0.2337 4365	0.2320 1183	4
5	0.1902 4686	0.1883 5457	0.1864 8137	0.1846 2711	0.1827 9164	0.1809 7480	5
6	0.1565 4997	0.1545 9750	0.1526 6821	0.1507 6190	0.1488 7839	0.1470 1747	6
7	0.1324 9543	0.1305 0635	0.1285 4449	0.1266 0961	0.1247 0147	0.1228 1982	7
8	0.1144 6735	0.1124 5639	0.1104 7665	0.1085 2783	0.1066 0965	0.1047 2181	8
9	0.1004 5689	0.0984 3386	0.0964 4601	0.0944 9299	0.0925 7447	0.0906 9008	9
10	0.0892 5876	0.0872 3051	0.0852 4137	0.0832 9094	0.0813 7882	0.0795 0457	10
11	0.0801 0596	0.0780 7745	0.0760 9197	0.0741 4904	0.0722 4818	0.0703 8889	11
12	0.0724 8713	0.0704 6209	0.0684 8395	0.0665 5217	0.0646 6619	0.0628 2541	12
13	0.0660 4827	0.0640 2954	0.0620 6157	0.0601 4373	0.0582 7535	0.0564 5577	13
14	0.0605 3652	0.0585 2634	0.0565 7073	0.0546 6897	0.0528 2032	0.0510 2397	14
15	0.0557 6646	0.0537 6658	0.0518 2507	0.0499 4110	0.0481 1381	0.0463 4229	15
16	0.0515 9899	0.0496 1085	0.0476 8483	0.0458 2000	0.0440 1537	0.0422 6991	16
17	0.0479 2777	0.0459 5253	0.0440 4313	0.0421 9852	0.0404 1758	0.0386 9914	17
18	0.0446 7008	0.0427 0870	0.0408 1684	0.0389 9333	0.0372 3690	0.0355 4622	18
19	0.0417 6062	0.0398 1388	0.0379 4033	0.0361 3862	0.0344 0734	0.0327 4501	19
20	0.0391 4713	0.0372 1571	0.0353 6108	0.0335 8175	0.0318 7614	0.0302 4259	20
21	0.0367 8733	0.0348 7178	0.0330 3659	0.0312 8011	0.0296 0057	0.0279 9611	21
22	0.0346 4661	0.0327 4739	0.0309 3207	0.0291 9881	0.0275 4565	0.0259 7051	22
23	0.0326 9638	0.0308 1390	0.0290 1880	0.0273 0906	0.0256 8249	0.0241 3682	23
24	0.0309 1282	0.0290 4742	0.0272 7283	0.0255 8683	0.0239 8703	0.0224 7090	24
25	0.0292 7592	0.0274 2787	0.0256 7404	0.0240 1196	0.0224 3903	0.0209 5246	25
26	0.0277 6875	0.0259 3829	0.0242 0540	0.0225 6738	0.0210 2137	0.0195 6432	26
27	0.0263 7687	0.0245 6421	0.0228 5241	0.0212 3854	0.0197 1946	0.0182 9189	27
28	0.0250 8793	0.0232 9323	0.0216 0265	0.0200 1298	0.0185 2081	0.0171 2253	28
29	0.0238 9127	0.0221 1467	0.0204 4538	0.0188 7993	0.0174 1461	0.0160 4551	29
30	0.0227 7764	0.0210 1926	0.0193 7133	0.0178 3010	0.0163 9154	0.0150 5144	30
31	0.0217 3900	0.0199 9893	0.0183 7240	0.0168 5535	0.0154 4345	0.0141 3212	31
32	0.0207 6831	0.0190 4662	0.0174 4150	0.0159 4859	0.0145 6320	0.0132 8042	32
33	0.0198 5938	0.0181 5612	0.0165 7242	0.0151 0357	0.0137 4453	0.0124 9004	33
34	0.0190 0675	0.0173 2196	0.0157 5966	0.0143 1477	0.0129 8191	0.0117 5545	34
35	0.0182 0558	0.0165 3929	0.0149 9835	0.0135 7732	0.0122 7045	0.0110 7171	35
36	0.0174 5158	0.0158 0379	0.0142 8416	0.0128 8688	0.0116 0578	0.0104 3446	36
37	0.0167 4090	0.0151 1162	0.0136 1325	0.0122 3957	0.0109 8402	0.0098 3979	37
38	0.0160 7012	0.0144 5934	0.0129 8214	0.0116 3192	0.0104 0169	0.0092 8423	38
39	0.0154 3615	0.0138 4385	0.0123 8775	0.0110 6083	0.0098 5567	0.0087 6462	39
40	0.0148 3623	0.0132 6238	0.0118 2728	0.0105 2349	0.0093 4315	0.0082 7816	40
41	0.0142 6786	0.0127 1241	0.0112 9822	0.0100 1738	0.0088 6158	0.0078 2229	41
42	0.0137 2876	0.0121 9167	0.0107 9828	0.0095 4020	0.0084 0868	0.0073 9471	42
43	0.0132 1688	0.0116 9811	0.0103 2539	0.0090 8989	0.0079 8235	0.0069 9333	43
44	0.0127 3037	0.0112 2985	0.0098 7768	0.0086 6454	0.0075 8071	0.0066 1625	44
45	0.0122 6751	0.0107 8518	0.0094 5343	0.0082 6246	0.0072 0202	0.0062 6173	45
46	0.0118 2676	0.0103 6254	0.0090 5108	0.0078 8205	0.0068 4471	0.0059 2820	46
47	0.0114 0669	0.0099 6051	0.0086 6919	0.0075 2189	0.0065 0734	0.0056 1421	47
48	0.0110 0599	0.0095 7777	0.0083 0646	0.0071 8065	0.0061 8858	0.0053 1843	48
49	0.0106 2348	0.0092 1314	0.0079 6167	0.0068 5712	0.0058 8722	0.0050 3965	49
50	0.0102 5806	0.0088 6549	0.0076 3371	0.0065 5020	0.0056 0215	0.0047 7674	50

n	2½%	3%	3½%	4%	4½%	5%	n
51	0.0099 0870	0.0085 3382	0.0073 2156	0.0062 5885	0.0053 3232	0.0045 2867	51
52	0.0095 7446	0.0082 1718	0.0070 2429	0.0059 8212	0.0050 7679	0.0042 9450	52
53	0.0092 5449	0.0079 1471	0.0067 4100	0.0057 1915	0.0048 3469	0.0040 7334	53
54	0.0089 4799	0.0076 2558	0.0064 7090	0.0054 6910	0.0046 0519	0.0038 6438	54
55	0.0086 5419	0.0073 4907	0.0062 1323	0.0052 3124	0.0043 8754	0.0036 6686	55
56	0.0083 7243	0.0070 8447	0.0059 6730	0.0050 0487	0.0041 8105	0.0034 8010	56
57	0.0081 0204	0.0068 3114	0.0057 3245	0.0047 8932	0.0039 8506	0.0033 0343	57
58	0.0078 4244	0.0065 8848	0.0055 0810	0.0045 8401	0.0037 9897	0.0031 3626	58
59	0.0075 9307	0.0063 5593	0.0052 9366	0.0043 8836	0.0036 2221	0.0029 7802	59
60	0.0073 5340	0.0061 3296	0.0050 8862	0.0042 0185	0.0034 5426	0.0028 2818	60
61	0.0071 2294	0.0059 1908	0.0048 9249	0.0040 2398	0.0032 9462	0.0026 8627	61
62	0.0069 0126	0.0057 1385	0.0047 0480	0.0038 5430	0.0031 4284	0.0025 5183	62
63	0.0066 8790	0.0055 1682	0.0045 2513	0.0036 9237	0.0029 9848	0.0024 2442	63
64	0.0064 8249	0.0053 2760	0.0043 5308	0.0035 3780	0.0028 6115	0.0023 0365	64
65	0.0062 8463	0.0051 4581	0.0041 8826	0.0033 9019	0.0027 3047	0.0021 8915	65
66	0.0060 9398	0.0049 7110	0.0040 3031	0.0032 4921	0.0026 0608	0.0020 8057	66
67	0.0059 1021	0.0048 0313	0.0038 7892	0.0031 1451	0.0024 8765	0.0019 7758	67
68	0.0057 3300	0.0046 4159	0.0037 3375	0.0029 8578	0.0023 7487	0.0018 7986	68
69	0.0055 6206	0.0044 8618	0.0035 9453	0.0028 6272	0.0022 6745	0.0017 8715	69
70	0.0053 9712	0.0043 3663	0.0034 6095	0.0027 4506	0.0021 6511	0.0016 9915	70
71	0.0052 3790	0.0041 9266	0.0033 3277	0.0026 3253	0.0020 6759	0.0016 1563	71
72	0.0050 8417	0.0040 5404	0.0032 0973	0.0025 2489	0.0019 7465	0.0015 3633	72
73	0.0049 3568	0.0039 2053	0.0030 9160	0.0024 2190	0.0018 8606	0.0014 6103	73
74	0.0047 9222	0.0037 9191	0.0029 7816	0.0023 2334	0.0018 0159	0.0013 8953	74
75	0.0046 5358	0.0036 6796	0.0028 6919	0.0022 2900	0.0017 2104	0.0013 2161	75
76	0.0045 1956	0.0035 4849	0.0027 6450	0.0021 3869	0.0016 4422	0.0012 5709	76
77	0.0043 8997	0.0034 3331	0.0026 6390	0.0020 5221	0.0015 7094	0.0011 9580	77
78	0.0042 6463	0.0033 2224	0.0025 6721	0.0019 6939	0.0015 0104	0.0011 3756	78
79	0.0041 4338	0.0032 1510	0.0024 7426	0.0018 9007	0.0014 3434	0.0010 8222	79
80	0.0040 2605	0.0031 1175	0.0023 8489	0.0018 1408	0.0013 7069	0.0010 2962	80
81	0.0039 1248	0.0030 1201	0.0022 9894	0.0017 4127	0.0013 0995	0.0009 7963	81
82	0.0038 0254	0.0029 1576	0.0022 1628	0.0016 7150	0.0012 5197	0.0009 3211	82
83	0.0036 9608	0.0028 2284	0.0021 3676	0.0016 0463	0.0011 9663	0.0008 8694	83
84	0.0035 9298	0.0027 3313	0.0020 6025	0.0015 4054	0.0011 4379	0.0008 4399	84
85	0.0034 9310	0.0026 4650	0.0019 8662	0.0014 7909	0.0010 9334	0.0008 0316	85
86	0.0033 9633	0.0025 6284	0.0019 1576	0.0014 2018	0.0010 4516	0.0007 6433	86
87	0.0033 0255	0.0024 8202	0.0018 4756	0.0013 6370	0.0009 9915	0.0007 2740	87
88	0.0032 1165	0.0024 0393	0.0017 8190	0.0013 0953	0.0009 5522	0.0006 9228	88
89	0.0031 2353	0.0023 2848	0.0017 1868	0.0012 5758	0.0009 1325	0.0006 5888	89
90	0.0030 3809	0.0022 5556	0.0016 5781	0.0012 0775	0.0008 7316	0.0006 2711	90
91	0.0029 5523	0.0021 8508	0.0015 9919	0.0011 5995	0.0008 3486	0.0005 9689	91
92	0.0028 7486	0.0021 1694	0.0015 4273	0.0011 1410	0.0007 9827	0.0005 6815	92
93	0.0027 9690	0.0020 5107	0.0014 8834	0.0010 7010	0.0007 6331	0.0005 4080	93
94	0.0027 2126	0.0019 8737	0.0014 3594	0.0010 2789	0.0007 2991	0.0005 1478	94
95	0.0026 4786	0.0019 2577	0.0013 8546	0.0009 8738	0.0006 9799	0.0004 9003	95
96	0.0025 7662	0.0018 6619	0.0013 3682	0.0009 4850	0.0006 6749	0.0004 6648	96
97	0.0025 0747	0.0018 0856	0.0012 8995	0.0009 1119	0.0006 3834	0.0004 4407	97
98	0.0024 4034	0.0017 5281	0.0012 4478	0.0008 7538	0.0006 1048	0.0004 2274	98
99	0.0023 7517	0.0016 9886	0.0012 0124	0.0008 4100	0.0005 8385	0.0004 0245	99
100	0.0023 1188	0.0016 4667	0.0011 5927	0.0008 0800	0.0005 5839	0.0003 8314	100

TABLE IV - SINKING FUND
Periodic deposit that will grow to $1 at future date

n	$5\frac{1}{2}\%$	6%	$6\frac{1}{2}\%$	7%	$7\frac{1}{2}\%$	8%	n
1	1.0000 0000	1.0000 0000	1.0000 0000	1.0000 0000	1.0000 0000	1.0000 0000	1
2	0.4866 1800	0.4854 3689	0.4842 6150	0.4830 9179	0.4819 2771	0.4807 6923	2
3	0.3156 5407	0.3141 0981	0.3125 7570	0.3110 5167	0.3095 3763	0.3080 3351	3
4	0.2302 9449	0.2285 9149	0.2269 0274	0.2252 2812	0.2235 6751	0.2219 2080	4
5	0.1791 7644	0.1773 9640	0.1756 3454	0.1738 9069	0.1721 6472	0.1704 5645	5
6	0.1451 7895	0.1433 6263	0.1415 6831	0.1397 9580	0.1380 4489	0.1363 1539	6
7	0.1209 6442	0.1191 3502	0.1173 3137	0.1155 5322	0.1138 0032	0.1120 7240	7
8	0.1028 6401	0.1010 3594	0.0992 3730	0.0974 6776	0.0957 2702	0.0940 1476	8
9	0.0888 3946	0.0870 2224	0.0852 3803	0.0834 8647	0.0817 6716	0.0800 7971	9
10	0.0776 6777	0.0758 6796	0.0741 0469	0.0723 7750	0.0706 8593	0.0690 2949	10
11	0.0685 7065	0.0667 9294	0.0650 5521	0.0633 5690	0.0616 9747	0.0600 7634	11
12	0.0610 2923	0.0592 7703	0.0575 6817	0.0559 0199	0.0542 7783	0.0526 9502	12
13	0.0546 8426	0.0529 6011	0.0512 8256	0.0496 5085	0.0480 6420	0.0465 2181	13
14	0.0492 7912	0.0475 8491	0.0459 4048	0.0443 4494	0.0427 9737	0.0412 9685	14
15	0.0446 2560	0.0429 6276	0.0413 5278	0.0397 9462	0.0382 8724	0.0368 2954	15
16	0.0405 8254	0.0389 5214	0.0373 7757	0.0358 5765	0.0343 9116	0.0329 7687	16
17	0.0370 4197	0.0354 4480	0.0339 0633	0.0324 2519	0.0310 0003	0.0296 2943	17
18	0.0339 1992	0.0323 5654	0.0308 5461	0.0294 1260	0.0280 2896	0.0267 0210	18
19	0.0311 5006	0.0296 2086	0.0281 5575	0.0267 5301	0.0254 1090	0.0241 2763	19
20	0.0286 7933	0.0271 8456	0.0257 5640	0.0243 9293	0.0230 9219	0.0218 5221	20
21	0.0264 6478	0.0250 0455	0.0236 1333	0.0222 8900	0.0210 2937	0.0198 3225	21
22	0.0244 7123	0.0230 4557	0.0216 9120	0.0204 0577	0.0191 8687	0.0180 3207	22
23	0.0226 6965	0.0212 7848	0.0199 6078	0.0187 1393	0.0175 3528	0.0164 2217	23
24	0.0210 3580	0.0196 7900	0.0183 9770	0.0171 8902	0.0160 5008	0.0149 7796	24
25	0.0195 4935	0.0182 2672	0.0169 8148	0.0158 1052	0.0147 1067	0.0136 7878	25
26	0.0181 9307	0.0169 0435	0.0156 9480	0.0145 6103	0.0134 9961	0.0125 0713	26
27	0.0169 5228	0.0156 9717	0.0145 2288	0.0134 2573	0.0124 0204	0.0114 4810	27
28	0.0158 1440	0.0145 9255	0.0134 5305	0.0123 9193	0.0114 0520	0.0104 8891	28
29	0.0147 6857	0.0135 7961	0.0124 7440	0.0114 4865	0.0104 9811	0.0096 1654	29
30	0.0138 0539	0.0126 4891	0.0115 7744	0.0105 8640	0.0096 7124	0.0088 2743	30
31	0.0129 1665	0.0117 9222	0.0107 5393	0.0097 9691	0.0089 1628	0.0081 0728	31
32	0.0120 9519	0.0110 0234	0.0099 9665	0.0090 7292	0.0082 2599	0.0074 5081	32
33	0.0113 3469	0.0102 7293	0.0092 9924	0.0084 0807	0.0075 9397	0.0068 5163	33
34	0.0106 2958	0.0095 9843	0.0086 5610	0.0077 9674	0.0070 1461	0.0063 0411	34
35	0.0099 7493	0.0089 7386	0.0080 6226	0.0072 3396	0.0064 8291	0.0058 0326	35
36	0.0093 6635	0.0083 9483	0.0075 1332	0.0067 1531	0.0059 9447	0.0053 4467	36
37	0.0087 9993	0.0078 5743	0.0070 0534	0.0062 3685	0.0055 4533	0.0049 2440	37
38	0.0082 7217	0.0073 5812	0.0065 3480	0.0057 9505	0.0051 3197	0.0045 3894	38
39	0.0077 7991	0.0068 9377	0.0060 9854	0.0053 8676	0.0047 5124	0.0041 8513	39
40	0.0073 2034	0.0064 6154	0.0056 9373	0.0050 0914	0.0044 0031	0.0038 6016	40
41	0.0068 9090	0.0060 5886	0.0053 1779	0.0046 5962	0.0040 7663	0.0035 6149	41
42	0.0064 8927	0.0056 8342	0.0049 6842	0.0043 3591	0.0037 7789	0.0032 8684	42
43	0.0061 1337	0.0053 3312	0.0046 4352	0.0040 3590	0.0035 0201	0.0030 3414	43
44	0.0057 6128	0.0050 0606	0.0043 4119	0.0037 5769	0.0032 4710	0.0028 0152	44
45	0.0054 3127	0.0047 0050	0.0040 5968	0.0034 9957	0.0030 1146	0.0025 8728	45
46	0.0051 2175	0.0044 1485	0.0037 9743	0.0032 5996	0.0027 9354	0.0023 8991	46
47	0.0048 3129	0.0041 4768	0.0035 5300	0.0030 3744	0.0025 9190	0.0022 0799	47
48	0.0045 5854	0.0038 9765	0.0033 2505	0.0028 3070	0.0024 0527	0.0020 4027	48
49	0.0043 0230	0.0036 6356	0.0031 1240	0.0026 3853	0.0022 3247	0.0018 8557	49
50	0.0040 6145	0.0034 4429	0.0029 1393	0.0024 5985	0.0020 7241	0.0017 4286	50

APPENDIX II

CREATING A FINANCIAL STATEMENT

CREATING A FINANCIAL STATEMENT

A financial statement is simply a list of your ASSETS (what you have) and a list of your LIABILITIES (what you owe). Banks have preprinted financial statements in which you simply fill in the blanks. I have always preferred to prepare my own statement in a way that makes sense to me.

On the opposite page is personal financial statement for Mr. Blue. Mrs. Blue is included because some assets are in both their names.

ASSETS are divided into QUICK ASSETS and OTHER ASSETS. Quick assets can be turned into cash in a day or two because there is an organized market for them such as the bond market or stock market.

NET WORTH is the difference between your ASSETS and your LIABILITIES.

It is customary to include the line TOTAL LIABILITIES AND NET WORTH as the last line in the statement before NOTES. Include in the NOTES anything that might affect your statement whether a plus or a minus. It is not necessary to include Annual Income in a Financial Statement.

This statement is very neatly set out and simple to understand. It indicates some degree of professionalism. In all my years of preparing Financial Statements, I have encountered only two institutions who, over my objections, required my statement to be adopted to their form. Somehow, I found it unnecessary to do business with them!

PERSONAL FINANCIAL STATEMENT
John S. Blue & Jane L. Blue
December 31, 1988

ASSETS

QUICK ASSETS

Cash in banks	$ 3,137	
Savings	98,432	
Stocks and bonds	15,669	
Gold coins	9,500	
TOTAL QUICK ASSETS		**$126,738**

OTHER ASSETS

Home	$ 65,000	
Automobiles	12,000	
Apartment house (8 units)	210,000	
TOTAL OTHER ASSETS		**$287,000**
TOTAL ASSETS		**$413,738**

LIABILITIES

Mortgage on home	$ 35,000	
Mortgage on Apartment house	135,000	
All other personal debts	5,000	
TOTAL LIABILITIES		**$175,000**
NET WORTH		**$238,738**
TOTAL LIABILITIES AND NET WORTH		**$413,738**

NOTES:
* Unsecured contingent liabilities - $ 3,000.
* Total life insurance in effect is $100,000.
* Annual income is in excess of $ 50,000.

Signed_____Date_____

APPENDIX III

GLOSSARY OF TERMS

Subsistence Level - Having an income sufficient to take care of your basic needs.

Option - Agreement to buy something in the future at specified terms and conditions.

Escrow - Money held under contract to be disbursed at a future date according to the terms and conditions of the contract.

Subordinate mortgage - To allow another mortgage to come before (ahead of) the Subordinated mortgage.

Construction loan - Interim mortgage to cover the period of construction and then replaced by the permanent mortgage.

Permanent loan - Same as permanent mortgage. Final loan to last until paid off over time.

Feasibility study - A study to determine if a project meets all regulations and is likely to meet the necessary profit criteria.

Pro forma operating statements - Financial projection of future profit and loss statements based on current expectations.